To Marti
with Best Wishes
Tom [illegible]

"The mind seeking freedom will never be comfortable with the seeming security of the immediate culture it is nourished by. It will seek to break out of its 'comfort corral' and view the larger expanse, so that it may grow."

--Athanasios

THE EQUATION
OF
ONE

--- *A LOGICAL TRIP TO A METAPHYSICAL CROSSROAD* ---

(Includes an appendix of select, metaphysically oriented poems.)

FIRST EDITION

Published and printed in the USA.

 For ordering books or for further information, please contact at e-mail address: TomLoizos@aol.com

Published by Tom Loizos
5901 So. 1300 East
Salt Lake City, UT 84121

ISBN 0-9658557-0-8

Library of Congress Catalogue Card Number: 97-93815

FOREWORD

-- by Athanasios

"And so, my son,

Have you really studied it out, or did you just memorize that which others have related to you, as 'The Truth?'

Just as in mathematics, my son, if you are to grow, the Truth must be solved by you and not for you. Who was it that said, 'Learn the Truth (for yourself) and the Truth will set you free?' And who is it that is tall enough now, to have you walk in their shadow?

You can learn the Truth, but you may need to start all over again, and with your own questions rather than from 'answers' possibly fed to you through love, fear or beliefs etc., or handed down by robed 'authorities.' Let no one, nor two or more, intimidate you into thinking you cannot solve the Truth for yourself.

My son - be not too proud, nor afraid to explore the thoughts presented to you - yet, let no one's light dazzle you. Bow to no one, nor to any organization, for your Godly light is within you, awaiting your understanding of it. You can do it now, for all that is holy is already within you. Let no one degrade you as 'man-made' and therefore incapable, for your real DNA is Godly.

Go forth, my son, in gratitude, gladness and love, but walk your own path, for another's may be flawed, no matter how well meant. Remember that dependency leads to more dependency. You have nothing to lose. Go forth in the light of your own, innate honesty and wisdom, and gain the understanding your soul is truly aspiring for."

TABLE OF CONTENTS

INTRODUCTION

When we are first born into this world, it seems that we are at the mercy of those who are taking care of us. Later we find that we exercise a strong control of our own, especially over our personal conditions. As we get older, however, we realize that our grip starts slipping, for our personal health starts to go. We also become more aware of the "oldness" in those about us. It is at this point that we either bow our heads in submission to "old age," or we seriously try to grasp the reins of life-control in order to restore our youth and the vitality that goes along with it.

Try as we might, no one has come up with the right answers for "eternal youth for everyone." Most of us have accepted the opposite idea which calls for "old age" and an earthly death as a necessity. If it was not for the idea that mortal death serves as the stepping stone into personal eternality, we would be sweating it out, anxiously searching for a valid answer. The accepting of the idea that we have someplace to go at the point of death is indeed comforting, and perhaps is the foundation upon which most religions stand. How many of us would be going to churches if we were experiencing the perpetuation of perfect health and perfect conditions in every way, including eternal youthfulness?

Belief in Christ is the manner in which many of us handle our uneasiness. There are those who would advise us thusly: "Establish faith in Christ, and when the axe finally falls, you will be lovingly resurrected and taken care of, for Christ has prepared a place for us.

He has promised to do this if we repent our wicked ways and believe in him as our Lord and Savior."

Yet, other religions teach that this is not a one-time bath into the fleshy presence, but we are reborn, time and time again, until we do learn the Truth and learn to live it. (Most of us are aware that there are other belief structures as well as those mentioned here.)

The fact that there are so many beliefs that "justify" our eternal validity, indicates how confused we are, and how desperate we are to convince ourselves of life after death.

In what direction should we proceed then? If we only knew someone personally, who knew enough to say; "Follow me, and I will not only talk, but I will show you what life and the eternal living of it, really is!" (We seem to be more in the act of demonstrating what a slow death is.)

It is with a sense of desperation then, that we proceed into the drama of life and death, especially since it involves the dying body that we have learned to identify as "me!" It is a subtle desperation, since dying involves a gradual depletion of health over many years in most cases. It is probably this same desperation that makes it easier for us to believe as true: "that which we want to be true," (and on somebody else's say-so, rather than researching it out for ourselves).

It is no wonder that religions whose boast is "eternal life for each personality," have gained such a following. The promise of eternal, personal identity! One wonders if it is the love of our fellow man and an interest in the good of all, or a fear based on personality extinction, that is the basis for the enduring quality of religions in our societies.

Some feel that we had no control of the factors involving our birth here. They feel that our destiny is under the control of whoever or whatever brought us here, and therefore: "If we have been produced by a power or force other than our own self, then that power is responsible for our well-being." Yet, other beliefs imply that since we are born with the ability of choice, it is our own responsibility to find out how to use that choice to guide our life into whatever enrichment is possible, including eternality. The implication is, that our "choice-power" overrules the choice of the greater power that "birthed" us here, therefore, it is up to us to determine our own future.

The key word in most religions seems to be "believe." But what about the words, "understand" and "demonstrate?" Demonstration would go a long way in setting an honest thinker at ease. But what is it going to take for us to be able to demonstrate the fact of "living," rather than the "fact" of "living and then dying?"

Some feel we can rely on modern science for guidance. Yet, modern science is still questioning whether they are dealing with consciousness or energy, or whether the two are actually the same thing! (Those who are really "in the scientific know," realize they are acquainted with much, but perhaps, <u>know</u> nothing.)

<u>Are</u> the reins of control in our hands, and, if we can determine that they are, what are our options? Will we be satisfied to remain in a comfort zone provided by the "Truths" of the particular religion

or society we are born into, or will we choose to strike out on our own?

This book is geared towards an in-depth presentation that will enable us to isolate and openly explore those concepts which are closest to our consciousness. However, we may wish to exercise caution in our appraisal of the new concepts offered, since the common procedure is to judge them by what we already believe rather than to examine them according to their own logical merit. A truly plausible justification for our individual being and its eternal existence as a personality, is no small undertaking.

The reader would do well to be aware of the bonds of loyalty and fear that bind him or her to family, race, religion and society. The true explorer realizes that the "old" must be left behind, if new territory is to be explored.*

---

* Throughout this book, all inference to gender applies equally to both women and men, regardless of the mode of its presentation.

SECTOR I

THE RELIGIOUS GRIP

RELIGIOUS COWBOY HAT

Is it true that we are proud, of "knowing where it's at,"
when all we may have ever done, is wear a cowboy hat
that parents and society have laid upon our head,
and questioned not, its meaning, until perhaps we're "dead?"

And did our parents really know their cowboy hat would fit?
And did they really care, as long as we would sit
just like a good and loyal dog, content to chew on bones
and fit into the pattern of some well-intentioned clones?

For if you wear a cowboy hat, "A cowboy you must be!"
and there's plenty more just like you, to keep you company.
They say that "You are one of us," and you may take great pride
in thinking just as they do, and be taken for a ride.

A horse is chosen for you, by those who "know much more,"
"and who are you to choose," when it's they who "know the score?"
And are they not exalted as knowing more than you,
because they've *memorized* what they and you should do?

To "seek and know the Truth through Self," is not repeated now;
"just listen to the story that we've *memorized* somehow,
and question not what's given you, and listen to 'just that,'
follow and obey the rules, (and wear your cowboy hat)!"

"And now that you're a cowboy, you stay inside your stall,
and don't you peek through the corral, or you will surely fall."
Be like the goodly Moslem, who kneels and bows each day,
in the given manner, when told that "it's the way."

(And if you think you're better, just look at where you sit -
were you branded by consent, or did you "just submit?")
If you want to be accepted, "tradition shows the way,"
and "the sacredness of our script," will tell you what to say - -

To bring more cowboys to the fold, you must be organized,
into a plan of telling, the "Truth" you've memorized.
So go out and knock on doors, and more will wear your brand,
(but before you tell another, have you *really* checked your hand?)

And if you don't obey, the rules of your corral,
the implication is, there's some sure kind of hell
awaiting you at death, but it's applied each day,
for ostracism plays its hand in very subtle ways.

The sword is not their weapon - its fear that's put to use
and it's their pecking order, that heaps on more abuse.
Guilt trips 'bout your children are another weapon too,
(but there's nothing more exalted, than the Truth you find for you.)

Deep down in their heart, each wants to do what's right
but are they strong enough to see that love's been spent as fright?
Can they forgive their loved ones, and those who helped them stay,
in the stifling corrals, while searching for the way?

"And so, my son,

Do you not realize that there are many levels of consciousness, each reflecting a differing realization of the Spirit? Why then should we be offended by the differences in Religions? Is not each level right for each who would accept it? If the garment fits the one who is wearing it, can it be improved upon? Be not dismayed, my son, for when the child outgrows the clothes it is wearing, it will seek out garments that do not bind."

--from the writings of Athanasios

CHAPTER I

ETERNALITY - A PROMISE

According to some versions of written history, the idea of eternality was handed down to us as an evolutionary progression. As one report has it, the Egyptian pharaohs of old "had it made," for they apparently were among the first to be "endowed" with everlasting life and allegedly had special temples built for their entombment. Eventually the high priests and priestesses managed to work their way into the "eternal fold." However, they had to be buried in "The Land of The Dead." Later on, as "capitalism" made a beach-head into the financial domain, anybody could have eternal life, but they too had to be buried in "The Land of The Dead." Of course, the price of burial lots didn't come cheap (Goats, sheep, camels, grain etc. were all acceptable as payment). Undoubtedly, no price was too high if you were assured of eternal life.

Then along came Jahweh! With the introduction of Jahweh, anybody could have eternal life. The only hitch was that there was also an eternal Hell for those who didn't behave in the prescribed moral manner. It doesn't take too much imagination to figure out how the masses would react to that! Eternality available to all? "Go with the flow!" All you had to do was "be good." Later on, divine forgiveness was widely accepted along with repentance, etc., for those who couldn't quite "cut the mustard."

Modern religions didn't cramp religious evolutionary style. One contemporary religion with its introduction of "three degrees of glory" rather than the radical "Heaven or Hell" situation, opened new doors. The severity of the punishment for crimes was reduced to a corrective status, while the rewards for being good still stood at full sail. A more lenient flow of direction towards eternality was welcomed with open arms.

Whether the historical versions of the reach for eternality are true or untrue, we can see that the idea of eternal life has always been of critical importance to mankind.

It is not the intent of this book to belittle or ridicule religion in any manner, since it is felt that each religion is originated in a spirit of enrichment for the level of consciousness it is introduced in, teaching self-responsibility in varying degrees. In that respect, no religion is doing wrong. Each of us, will progress to higher and higher levels of Self-realization. As we learn to "fly" we will outgrow the nests of beliefs we have frequented, and reach for an *understanding* of the Self we call "I."

It is the intent of this book to reveal how our presence in this universe *is* of a Divine nature, that presently is widely misunderstood. Though religions have possibly served each of us with that which we were ready for, many honest natures are seeking beyond the limited concepts thrust upon them and want to *understand* who and what they really are for themselves, rather than to remain in a position of *believing* what somebody else tells them. They sense that dependency can only lead to more dependency. In order to progress, we must arrive at the point where religions are understood to be our servant rather than our master. It is essential that we learn how to think, rather than be taught what to think.

Probably, every religion that has ever existed has served to acquaint mankind, in one way or another, with the idea of a spiritual heritage and presence, as opposed to a mere animalistic or a mechanical existence. In a world of selfishness and "self-importance," most religions have endeavored to establish ideas of altruism and conscientious behavior. In many cases, however, their adherents have become clannish and of a "closed-mind" nature. Too many have been fenced in by the religion they were born into, to such a degree that they seek no further for the Truth.

Religions do not seem to be very fond of "graduation exercises." How many have come up with the message: "You have learned all we can teach you, and now the time has come to leave the nest and try out your own wings"? Our poem which precedes this chapter is designed to show us how good intentions can work against us if they are not governed by wisdom.

In some of the Far-Eastern religious cultures, full self-responsibility has been taught for centuries: "The consequences you sow are the consequences you yourself shall reap."

The fact is, you are answerable to Self and not to a separate "overlord" called "God." This is hinted at in the Moslem, Judaic and Christian cultures and is, perhaps, openly approached in the Christian Science religion and in some of the organizations branching off from that religion.

Ancient, as well as modern metaphysical circles, have indicated that self is fully responsible to Self for its actions, i.e., answerable to Self, only. A higher Self than the eroding, physical self we now identify ourselves as, is not only hinted at in this text, but is logically established as the reality of *all* being.

The position most of us find ourselves in is, that we have either surrendered our minds to the beliefs of a religion that is acceptable to us, or we are living in a questioning atmosphere, honestly admitting that we are not sure. Most are willing to give some attention to solving the mystery of their presence for themselves but don't know how to go about it.

The understanding of the difference between "infinite" and "eternal" is essential to those who are truly interested in finding out just who and what we really are. This difference is elaborated on in the chapters to follow.

SECTOR II

IS THERE A GOD?

"IN A NUTSHELL"

For years scientists have been puzzled by a question regarding beehives and bees. "Is each bee an entity in itself, or is each hive itself, the entity and the bees merely its 'cells' acting much as the cells do in our body, except that the 'bee-cells' have wings and can leave and return at will?"

Modern day cloning processes have proven that each cell in each human body contains the exact image of the whole of the body as it currently is. This issue is further demonstrated by the healing processes of wounds on our bodies. Whenever we cut ourselves, the rebuilding of the wound stops when the current image of the body is once more restored, rather than the rebuilding continue indefinitely like a growing branch on a tree. The cells apparently cognize the overall unity they are a part of and know when to stop the rebuilding process.

Undoubtedly each bee also realizes the overall unity it belongs to. Just as the cells in our body function to establish protection, nourishment, renewal and restoration, etc., the bees function similarly. Because of their wings and greater freedom, they apparently enjoy a grander vista of presence, but it does not stop them from their supporting role.

Is it possible that each bee, like each human cell, holds the full image of the hive it supports? Is it possible that each bee thinks that it IS that hive-identity itself, and that is why it innately serves to support and unify that hive as if it were itself? Some might say this would be impossible, yet this is apparently what is happening in the case of human cells. Each one of your cells thinks it is your entire body - you - but in accordance with its own level of self-realization.

The consciousness of "oneness-of-identity" throughout each body is what maintains it as a functioning unity. Each cell thinks it IS you! Otherwise each cell would be living off of your body as a parasite rather than contributing to it as a singular identity. This apparently is true of all species of life.

This book is dedicated to showing how the obscurity of God can be cleared up by presenting God as what God really is: The all-encompassing "hive" of Infinite Consciousness (The Infinite Self), wherein we are the "bees" sharing the identity of the Whole according to individual levels of Self-realization. Each of us is accustomed to identifying ourselves as "I," and everyone else as a separate identity - a separate "I." We are actually shown how we all share the same identity - the same "I," similar to the example of the bees and the beehive. The mistaken concept that God is a separate identity is dispelled.

An overall "Whole-control" is proven rather than surmised. How this "Whole-control" we have named "God," works through us towards the enrichment of the Whole is also illustrated.

Through ignorance and fear, the name "God" has been abused for centuries. Rather than to portray it as our True Self, it has been portrayed as a separate self, and in a ridiculous pose in many cases. Because of this, any mention of God or religion is immediately avoided by many thinkers, and understandably so.

Introduced in this text will be the <u>understanding</u> of what is meant by the statement, "God is infinite." One of the vital steps into a higher understanding of Self is the gaining of a comprehensive realization of what "infinite" implies.

God, as infinite life is shown to be a progression. This means the "tapes" can be rolled back for a view of "God in infancy." Step by step illustrations of the God progression is a key part of this presentation, since they will show how we are involved. The word "infinite" will be derived, as will the meanings of "eternal," "cognition" (elemental consciousness) and "re-cognition" (relativity). Many of us will meet with issues that are new to us, including the derivation of the fact that ALL is composed of consciousness.

At the moment, the direction of this presentation may seem to be far out, at least to the reader who may not be acquainted with a research so demanding of reason and logic. However, it is not beyond the scope of each of us to grasp an elemental understanding of who and what we are. It is indeed fascinating to finally find a reasonable explanation regarding our births and our presence. We may be pleasantly surprised to see how the puzzle comes together as we explore the issues involved.

"And so, my son,

Is not your body more than the sum of its parts? Think, my son, could a box filled with all your human parts be of any use, or is there more to you than a collection of your parts? If there is more to your wholeness than your parts, what is it we have overlooked? Is it not the overall control which integrates them into a functioning oneness? Is it not "whole control" that we have overlooked?

And is not The Infinite Whole then also, more than the sum of its parts? A child, my son, can see that it is. The Whole is more than the sum of its parts because it includes the overall control of them. Without an overall Whole-control, a Whole is not whole, but merely complete - a collection of pieces."

--from the writings of Athanasios

CHAPTER II

THE PROOF OF GOD AS A REALITY

The German word "gestalt" literally implies that The Whole is more than the sum of its parts, and with good reason, as shown by the comments of Athanasios. The fact that The Whole is more than the sum of its parts is self-evident. If it was less than the sum of its parts it would, of course, not be whole. If it was limited to the sum of its parts it would be complete but still would not be *whole*. To observe that there is more to The Whole than the sum of its parts is indeed an astute observation. Yes, The Whole *is* more than the sum of its parts because The Whole includes the controlling unification through which, not only The Whole has meaning, but through which every part attains its appropriate significance. (Without a whole, a part would be of no significance, since it depends upon the whole for its purpose.)

If "ALL that is," is "The Whole," then for the same reasons as given above, it must include an overall, unifying control. This supreme control of "all that is," is what the world intuitively has sensed, and named "God." Throughout the primitive ages, to the more sophisticated age we live in now, God apparently, has always been sensed as an abstract reality. Always a mystery, this reality is just now reaching the point of tangible presentation.

One may question that the Whole *is* composed of parts. Yet, if the Whole was a homogenous mass (the only other alternative), it would still require control to maintain that standard. There would still be a supreme control. However, a homogenous mass does not leave much room for progression. It will be illustrated in chapters to follow, that whatever else God is, God is Life. It will be shown that all life, with no exceptions, is in the state of progression. Nothing is static.

One might ask, "What proof is there, if I am a part, that there *is* a Whole?" A part could not be nor exist unless there was a Whole to belong to. A part must be a part-of *something*. If there was no Whole there would be nothing to be a part *of*! If there is a part, this of course proves then that there is a Whole. And if there is a Whole, this proves that there is a control of the Whole, since a Whole cannot *be* without an overall control. Otherwise, as mentioned above, it would be but a collection of parts. This shows us then that The Whole is a reality. It also shows us that The Whole, to be whole, must be unified under one control. This is the logic that proves that there is a God - one supreme control of all that is (The Whole).

Rather than to recognize that God *is* and to try and analyze out how, what and who it is and how it operates, it has been common practice to conceptualize God in terms of power that is respected or feared, or to portray God as a sort of super-human. If we were ants, God would probably be conceptualized as a "super-ant." There are some religions that do name God "Spirit" or "Love," which is a step in the right direction, except that "Spirit" and "Love" are not tangibly derived.

One of the objectives of this treatise, is to understandably illustrate what God really is, and how God is progressing. God is portrayed for what God is: The Infinite Presence. How an Infinite Presence could have "a beginning and a progression" is indeed a challenging issue. However the Godly progression is portrayed in a step by step manner, as is the part we play in it.

We must be careful not to make the mistake that many have, in blandly accepting the idea that we are God's creation, and that somehow God created us out of nothing. No matter how you cut it, only nothingness can come from nothingness. This mistaken "core-concept" has led many astray, confusing the clarity of the reasoning in which true answers lie. Hopefully our presentation about the issues governing our origin, will dispel this belief and with a clarity of reasoning, show what is happening and why. We must all eventually learn to trust our honesty to guide us rather than the explanations of those who perhaps were misled by others, and who, desperately grasping for answers, reached out for the best they could find in order to allay their fears and ignorance. The results of our explorations based upon tangible reasoning lie before us. Hopefully, most will examine them fearlessly and with the openness of mind they deserve.

"I only hope it comes to be,
that the hand of God focussed as "me,"
prevails unto maturity
as a guiding light for "we."

--Athanasios

THE HAND OF GOD

The child's face glows with a smile
and radiates love - and it stares for a while
with wonder filled eyes, as it plays in the sand.
Could it be, its aware of the touch of God's hand?

Across the street, his money he counts -
the beggar - measures his worth by amounts
of coin he's secured, in a generous land
where all is sustained by the touch of God's hand -

a Grace that the beggar's not yet defined -
except perhaps, in the progressing mind
of the child within him, an entity grand,
that lives in the realm of God's guiding hand.

That arrogant look, remote and discreet,
displayed on the faces of some folks we meet
is fear-filled aloofness, defensively bland
(yet, behind the mask, is the touch of God's hand).

Resentment, anger and fear make their play,
in the selfish outlook some would portray -
yet innate to each, like the crystal in sand
is the ever abiding, touch of God's hand - -

Pride or vanity, or sheer selfishness
claiming residence at our address
can't overshadow the fact that we stand
always, inside the grip of God's hand.

Those hearts filled, not with love, but with hate
will find one day, that the storms of that fate
evolve into love that they'll understand;
for each is endowed, with the touch of God's hand.

Mistaken action - all we've done wrong -
repeats itself 'til it "just don't belong,"
and each who has grown at wisdom's command
knows we've been blessed with the touch of God's hand.

Infinite Grace can never be lost
to an immature posture that we accost
in our experience - woman or man -
for guiding us each, is the touch of God's hand.

SECTOR III

IS CONSCIOUSNESS *ALL* THAT IS?

"And so, my son,

Do you not realize that the more you progress in error, the deeper your footsteps will become mired? Yes, you can build a complete house using the mistaken concept: 2+2=5. You will find that the roof will probably leak, and the wind may blow through the walls, although additional patchwork will cover errors as they become apparent. The older the house gets, the more dilapidated it will become, and more patchwork will become necessary.

And what about our lives? Is it not apparent that the more we progress in "what we know," the older our bodies get, and the more dilapidated they become, with more patchwork necessary to maintain their functions? How many wear eyeglasses? How many use walking supports? Hearing aids? How many heart bypasses have restored weakened circulation to tolerable levels? Are not most doctors and hospitals involved with repair work? How many drug stores does our society support? What is all this telling us?

My, son, if the first concept you proceed from is in error, all that follows must also suffer from the same error, for nothing that is right can ever proceed from that which is originally wrong. One of our problems is that the more we become acquainted with error, the more we think we know about Truth, and thereby continue even deeper into degradation. Is it not critical for us to stop now, and question the merit of those first concepts we have accepted as Truth?"

--from the writings of Athanasios

"Animals function primarily through the use of their instinct and their senses of hearing, seeing, touching, tasting and smelling, do they not? If we do not take time to reason, can we expect to rise much higher than animals on the scale of intelligence?"

--Athanasios

CHAPTER III

CONSCIOUSNESS, THE ONLY SUBSTANCE

As incredible as it may seem, *consciousness is the only substance there actually is.* Regardless of what we name it, be it "consciousness," "awareness," "mind," "spirit," "matter," or even something exotic like, "the ethereal," there is no other substance in the whole of the universe. *There is nothing else*. This fact has probably never been fully understood. Because of this, the thinking of mankind has been handicapped for centuries.

To explore the reasoning behind our statements, we shall involve a law that most of us can agree with: *"It takes something whose substance is solidity to move something else whose substance is also solidity."* This simply says, that it takes something solid to move something that's solid. Using the same reasoning then, we can also say: *"A substance whose essence and nature is one of non-solidity, can never touch nor move a substance whose essence and nature is solidity."* In other words, if your body was made out of a "ghostly" substance with no solidity (like we see portrayed in some movies), it could glide right through walls. Your hands could not even pick up anything so simple as a glass of water, since they would be without any solidity whatsoever, and therefore would pass right through it. *Its important to realize then, that for one thing to even so much as touch another thing, it has to be of the same essence as the other*. In summation then: *"The movement of one thing by another can only be achieved by something that is of the same basic essence and nature."*

Yet when we raise our arm, our consciousness, whose nature is non-solidity, has moved our arm, which apparently is of a solid nature. How do we account for this?

It is our reasoning that forces us to acknowledge that the simple raising of our hand *at the command of our consciousness* proves that consciousness and our hand must both be composed of the same substance and are therefore, of the same nature and essence. If they were not, one of them could never move the other, as indicated by the above given law, that states: *"In order for one thing to be moved by something else, only something that is of the same basic essence and nature can do so."* As incredible as it may seem, this means that our body which is *controlled* by consciousness, must then be *composed* of consciousness. This is the realization, as simple as it may be, that mankind has failed to acknowledge. Had this been observed, acknowledged and studied, the whole thinking structure of humankind would have been changed. We would be treating our bodies with remedies of correct thinking and feeling, rather than with medicines. Instead of our bodies "telling us how we feel," we would be telling our bodies how "they" feel. Instead of our bodies "mastering" us, we would be mastering our bodies. Undoubtedly, the day will come when "The Science of True Being," and "The Science of Harmonious Living" will become basic sciences in our academic learning curriculums. (Grade school level would certainly not be out of place for such a teaching.)

Our concerns about the essence of our bodies is important, but our explorations lead us into even deeper water, since they involve the whole of the universe. If the raising of our hand at the command of consciousness proves that our hand is composed of consciousness, what does it tell us when the hand is commanded to pick up a book that is laying on a table? If the hand that's composed of consciousness can grasp the book, then the book also has to be of the same substance: Consciousness! And the table that holds up the book? This also has to be consciousness! And the world that supports the table? Consciousness! And the universe that houses the world? Consciousness!

Perhaps the seeming simplicity through which we raise our hand has caused us to overlook the terrible significance of such an act. The fact, *that anything your hand can touch or affect has to be consciousness*, will take some getting used to. Yet, there is a very intelligent reason why things are the way they are, as our progressing exploration will show us.

Up to this point, we have shown that because consciousness moves and controls our body, they both must be of one and the same substance. We have not overlooked the other side of the coin which says, "What if they are both composed of matter?" We see that this is impossible when we realize that matter, in and of itself, cannot command and is therefore, incapable of control. Matter can only "obey" the apparent laws of gravity, magnetism and inertia, and other Newtonian type laws. It is not in a command situation. *It can only respond, therefore cannot initiate action, since it is incapable of doing so.* If "matter-substance" was the reality of the universe, you would see the forces of inertia, gravity and magnetism, slowly bringing everything into a mechanical balance - from the stars to every minute speck of dust. The dominant forces of gravity, magnetism and inertia, etc., would eventually push and pull everything into its place, and the universe would come to a stationary rest in a sort of mechanical equilibrium. It would be kind of like a magnet surrounded by iron filings. The magnetism would attract each filing, placing it into a patterned structure. Once that balance was established, there would be no more change initiated, since all movement would be arrested in that power structure. There would be no spontaneous action, for everything and everyone would respond only to the mechanical placement of the balanced forces of inertia, gravity, and magnetism, etc.

It is consciousness, (choice, desire, will, motive, etc.) that picks us up from the chairs we sit on. Otherwise we would be sitting there - forever locked in place by the balancing grip of the forces depicted above. What else other than consciousness could or would initiate changes? *The fact that we can raise our bodies up from the chairs we sit on, proves that it is consciousness that is the essence of the universe.* (Matter is actually "structured consciousness." This will be elaborated on as we progress.)

Life as we experience it, is kind of like dream-consciousness. Each dreamer manufactures everything in their dreams according to the concepts of consciousness they believe to be real, be they of solidity, pain, pleasure, etc. But everything in the dream, regardless of how it is experienced or interpreted, is actually a formation structured *from* dream-consciousness. Our normal, waking, life experience falls into a comparable category. We cannot change the "consciousness-essence" of our everyday experiences by misinterpreting them as materialistic, no more than we can change the "consciousness-essence" of our dreams. It is apparent that consciousness is the essence of both our dream life and our normal, everyday life. If you could somehow extract the consciousness from them, everything would immediately vanish, like when you turn off your television. Consciousness is the essence of all.

Some may postulate that matter and consciousness might coexist. Though we have covered this to some extent, we will review it a bit because it is important that there is no confusion in our minds regarding the impossibility of this taking place. If matter was a structure of non-consciousness, it would be incapable of self control, or of being controlled by consciousness. It would have no facilities to receive or acknowledge control of any kind. Only consciousness can know of control, or control-commands, *since commands can only register on consciousness.* The fact is, only consciousness can control, and be controlled. (As has been abundantly presented, if matter and consciousness were each of a different essence, they could not even touch each other, let alone control or be controlled by one or the other. The co-existence of both of them is an impossibility.)

Matter, as a sovereign substance in and of itself, is an impossibility. Matter can only exist as a function of consciousness. It is actually structured consciousness, being used to fulfill the tangibility requirements of progressing intelligence. (The function called matter and its purpose is fully presented as we progress further into our study.) If there was such a thing as a non-consciousness such as the matter belief portrays, it could not sustain its own presence since it could be conscious of nothing. (Even a drop of water knows when it should sustain itself as a liquid, when it should boil or freeze, or when it should evaporate. Without consciousness this would be impossible).

In the interest of further clarification, we would make note that consciousness, in and of itself, is not intelligence. Intelligence is the control of consciousness. This control is inherent in consciousness itself and will be one of our more important issues to be explored, in fact, every element of consciousness will receive a close scrutiny.

It has indeed been a challenge to show that it is strictly consciousness and its ramifications that we are dealing with. Even with the consideration that it is our awareness and nothing else that we function with in our utilization of the objective universe, it is hard for us to get away from the idea of matter as a reality. There is much yet to be introduced regarding this, to show us what the situation actually is and why it had to be that way.

It has probably been even more of a challenge for the scientific community to try and prove the false concept that matter, in and of itself is a reality with properties of its own, what with the discovery of quarks, neutrinos, anti-matter particles, etc. According to scientific tests as reported in his enlightening book, "The Dancing Wu Li Masters," Gary Zukav points out, how in documented, scientific experiments with "matter particles," the results were changed merely by the perception of them. Experiments of this nature will help corroborate the fact that it is only consciousness that we are dealing with.

SECTOR IV

EVOLUTION

"And so, my son,

You have read the Scriptures have you not? 'God spoke and form appeared.' Do you believe it, my son? Do you really believe that 'someone speaks and form appears' or do you think there's another explanation? For the simple childlike mind, this might do, but a mature thinker realizes that even a God could not make something out of nothing. It is impossible, my son, to get somethingness out of an absolute nothingness, just as it is impossible to make an absolute nothingness out of a somethingness. My son, everything that is, always was, and always will be.

Although it has generally been assumed so, let us point out that the Scriptures do not specifically say that form did appear out of a nothingness. Those who would believe so, do not understand the process of synthesis which is accomplished through a realization process. However, was mankind prepared to understand such a process at the time Genesis was written? And you, my son - are you ready to look at 'creation' from a realistic standpoint?"

--from the writings of Athanasios

"Before a task can be completed, it must first be begun. And how many times has error surfaced, due to a mis-taken first step? And yet, if that first step had not been taken, would the correct way have ever come to light?"

--Athanasios

CHAPTER IV

EVOLUTION

It was Darwin who submitted his "Origin of Species" to a Truth-hungry world. This was a lifetime achievement of painstaking research and a great testimonial to his dedication. Every stepping stone in our progression has its place and just so, his works have served us. However, had Darwin realized that the basic essence of all is consciousness, it is very probable that his explorations and conclusions would have taken a different turn. The idea that matter, in and of itself, is capable of progression is an assumption based upon error. Activity can only occur under the auspices of consciousness.

The study of what we *see* does have its place, but we must be cautious in the drawing of conclusions based solely on the study of "what we see." As an example, the evolution of life is not a condition of "the survival of the fittest," but is a condition of "the abundance of The Whole," as will soon be explained. The Whole is not "surviving" in any manner, but is already "completely established and fully fit." It is in a continual state of progression and always has been. That which is commonly called "evolution," does depict life's advancement, but when understood rightly, will be seen as the progression of The Whole into a higher realization of Self.

To talk about "the evolution of consciousness" and "the progression of consciousness" in the same breath could be a bit confusing. There is a difference. They both indicate change, and both imply a step by step advance into a higher stage of development. The difference between the two is in how the higher development occurs. As an example, one of the fundamental concepts of evolution is the implication that a lower species of something, in and of itself, can develop into a higher species. The idea that a "lesser species," in and of itself, can develop into more than what it essentially is, is a mistaken concept. This (if we may use an analogy), is like saying that if a penny was a form of life, then it, in and of itself, could eventually progress into becoming a dollar. To see how impossible this is, let us imagine that there is nothing else except for that one penny. Now if a penny is the only thing there is, how could it ever develop into more than what it essentially is? Where will it get its direction from, to become more than that which is housed within it? Where will the idea of nickel, dime, quarter, etc., come from if those ideas and all that they imply were not already housed within it, to guide it into higher progression? Can it produce new ideas out of nothingness? We have already portrayed the impossibility of getting "somethingness" out of nothingness.[1] However, if the penny represented the consciousness of a whole dollar that was living in a lower state of self-realization, then it could and would, progress through all its lower states. It would first experience its penny life, and then progress through the nickel, dime and quarter experiences,

[1] *In our presentation, we accept as self-evident the fact that "somethingness" can never emanate from an absolute nothingness, nor can a "somethingness" ever be made into a nothingness.*

etc. until it achieved the wholeness that it innately was all the time. The lower species would not have become a higher species - the higher species was there all the time, progressing towards its highest realization. All that is and ever will be of anything, is totally included in its essence, even though it may be abiding in its lowest degree of presence. Innate within every presence is The Whole, regardless of the degree of development.

One of the realizations that Darwin was undoubtedly seeking, is the truth that *evolution is actually a process of the whole state of being experiencing all of its lower states progressively, until it achieves the full understanding of what it wholly is.* Evolution is not, and has not ever been initiated by a "lower" species nor any so called "part" of life. All evolution is initiated by The Whole, towards achieving a full understanding of Self.

To further clarify the real action of evolution, let us use an acorn in another analogy. Without the whole of an oak tree already ingrained in its essence, the acorn could never become the oak tree. If we could somehow watch the individual development of the acorn cells with our normal eyesight, it would be easy to say that lower species of cells were developing into higher species of cells as they changed into more complex forms. However, it is now plain that what we would be seeing is "the whole" - the oak tree itself, in the state of becoming.

There is no independent action of "parts." Because we have not outgrown our strong dependency on outer perception, we commonly make the mistake of believing that a part is separate from the Whole, and can thereby act independently. As indicated, the whole of everything always is. If it "wasn't," there would be no end product available - no"blueprint" - nothing to impel and guide progression towards eventual fulfillment. A part therefore, cannot progress independent of the whole. (Even if a part could somehow become independent from its whole, it would lose its meaning, even as an isolated piece of a picture-puzzle without the whole of the puzzle, would have no place else to fit into.) This means, of course, that if we are parts, then we too are parts of The Whole, with all that is implied herein, applicable to our lives.

We can now see to some extent how The Whole is in command of all progression, subtle as that control may be. This will be further expounded upon as we proceed. Everything progresses in the pattern established by "whole-presence." Progression without an innate "blueprint of The Whole," is impossible. Whether we name it "evolution" or "progression" does not matter. It is important for us to be aware of what is actually happening, since this will assist us to better understand subsequent presentations.

It is also important for us to realize, that if all action is contained in The Whole and controlled by The Whole, so called "independent mutations" cannot occur. The Whole is all that wholeness implies. There is nothing, without. It includes all, even the so called "mutations." For whatever reason it does so, progression follows the given pattern. All so called "mutations" are innate - within The Whole. There can be no "accidents" in Life.

Most of us have probably made the mistake of relying too heavily on our "outer" perceptions. We would do well to rely more upon our basic reasoning rather than upon what we see. (As you can tell from what you've studied so far, it is not quite so simple, but if you didn't have a true hunger for Truth and freedom you would never have come this far.) It is indeed fascinating to explore beneath the surface.

You may have noticed the emphasis we have placed upon the word "understanding" throughout this chapter. The understanding of who and what we are is ever our goal. Beliefs are but leaning posts that we use along the way. (It is one thing to get into a car, turn on the key and to believe it is going to move. It is something else to get into it with the *understanding* of the workings of the internal combustion engine and all that is actually happening to control energy so that it can be used for transportation purposes. It is one thing to believe that the soap you put into a wash machine will work to loosen the dirt from the clothes. It is another thing to *understand* the chemical principles that govern the action of the ingredients that soap is made from.) Yes, there is a great deal of difference between just believing something to be true and the actual understanding of that truth!

The understanding of Self, is the present focus of our life progression. Apparently there is nothing born in this earthly realm as an "understood self." Life knows Self, in fact is all-knowing, but has to undergo relative experience in order to understand its Self. That is what we are doing here, in our earthly existence.

Our next two chapters, "Sex," and, "The Infinite," deal with Whole-presence as a constancy within and throughout all. Hopefully, this chapter has prepared us to understand why the presence of The Whole is ever with us.

SECTOR V

SEX

FLESH AND BONES

Skeletons that walk on earth,
with flesh that clings like clothes, at birth -
fleshy pleasure - fleshy pain
memories housed in a fleshy brain.

Fleshy clothes on human bones
that identify the clones -
see the fleshy evidence
of identity and scent.

And the grip of flesh on bones
provides a signature in tones -
a temporal identity,
established as a "he" or "she" -

and the image we embrace,
presents to us, a changing face.
What is our <u>true</u> identity?
Who is the "I," I call a me?

(And what is it that moves the bones?
What satisfaction cries and moans
for a carnal fulfillment -
flesh for an attirement?)

"And so, my son,

Have you not heard the call? 'Have Faith!' And have you not wondered about Faith? Faith, my son, is the name of the feeling: 'certainty-realization.' Your Faith is the certainty-realization you feel about the reality that is you. When you rise up out of your chair, it is your Faith that you are utilizing. Perhaps it is so common to you that you are unaware of it: the Faith, 'I am, I can, I do!' If you did not have the Faith that you could rise up out of your chair you would remain there indefinitely unless someone or something else moved you. My son, if someone invites you to trust them, it is because they feel you don't have enough Faith in them - that you are uncertain of them. It is only when you are not certain, that trust is required.

And how many of us have put our trust in God? What does this tell us? Does this not say that our understanding is not clear - that questions still abide?

My son, it is not a question of 'having' Faith, for you are innately endowed with ALL of the richness of being. However, not being fully aware of all that we truly are, we are prone to misplace our feeling of certainty-realization. Has this not been the case? Would it not be wise to better acquaint ourselves with our Godly heritage?"

--from the writings of Athanasios

CHAPTER V

SEX

If included, this subject is usually reserved for the latter part of most books. In this text however, we shall open the door earlier. The understanding of what sex actually is, is vital to the student of life and involves the presence of every living thing in this universe. Hopefully, this journey into a world of concepts so foreign to everyday beliefs will not scare away too many students. If this does get too deep and confusing, the reader is advised to skip over this chapter and come back to it later.

Sex? That which we call sex is actually the synthesizing force of the universe. It is not the act of creating, as creation is *commonly* understood. When two humans copulate, it is not sex. It is the result of sex. Sex is the force that urges two people to copulate.

Cell division normally begins when a female egg is fertilized by the male sperm and is the apparent action where one cell divides itself into two cells, both of which are a duplication of the original. This duplicating action does not stop with the first two cells, but is a continuing process that normally results in the birth of offspring. There is, however, more to cell division than the action mentioned above. Cell division in and of itself is impossible. Without heat, a cell would remain unchanged. Heat must be furnished in order for cell division to transpire. Heat is a manifestation of energy. Energy is "that which is the essence of all action." Our question then must be, "Exactly what, is the essence of all action?" If we solve the answer to that question, we will understand what the synthesizing force of the universe is - we will know what sex really is.

The synthesizing force of the universe! We are talking about the force that established the first formation, ever. This mystery has somehow touched all of us, but most of us probably feel we are not ready to handle it and usually settle for one or another of the various religious beliefs. Most religions ascribe all initial action to the God they present as "The Creator." Others would say that creation is established by intelligence. The word "intelligence" is commonly used as a sort of blanket term, just as many people use the word, "God." We are prone to use those terms when we cannot reasonably explain the origin of something. However, unless terms are *tangibly* derived, they tend to leave us with a sense of mystery. Creation need not be a mystery to those who are ready to understand it, but like the learning of higher mathematics, an understanding of basic fundamentals must first be attained.

We have touched upon many basic fundamentals, but one of the most important is the concept that consciousness is not "a," but "*the*" basic and only action. It is from this basic *action* that all transpires. To the casual reader, this may seem "far out" since most of us have probably never considered the possibility that "action" itself is the life-substance, let alone the only substance there is! Most of us feel that matter is a medium through which force acts, not realizing that matter itself, is actually a formation of action. It is "action" that we must gain an understanding of, if we are to understand life. Matter is the result of action.[2] We are so accustomed to the *apparent* "form activity" about us that many of us have assumed that matter has its own laws and even its own type of

---

[2] *It is interesting to note that the theories of Einstein reduce matter, not to space and time, but to a position of space-time, dependent upon how our consciousness views it in terms of space position and in terms of time position.*

volition. [As strange as it may seem, our dreams perhaps give us a more realistic sense of the idea of "action as a substance" than does our everyday life. Everything in our dreams is structured from action (our consciousness) and lives and moves in that action. As we proceed, we will see how all that is, abides in action, as action.]

What has all this got to do with sex? A whole lot, if we are to *understand* what sex actually is. A new ground work must be clearly established in our own mind, especially regarding the structure of consciousness, since without consciousness there would be no life. Sex is a function of consciousness, and not of our bodies, as we may have previously thought.

Somewhere in the richness of his truly, informative books, Thomas Troward expounded on the principle that "a lie is something which 'is not,' therefore the Truth is all there *actually* is." As we are presenting it in this text, the word "Truth" (that which actually is), relates to activity rather than a variety of facts stored in limbo, like a deck of cards awaiting play. All Truth is in constant use, in fact, it is perpetual action. Action means "doing something" as opposed to the concept of a deathly stillness.

The basic fundamental action of The Infinite Wholeness, is its timeless, "Whole-Cognition." Because the Infinite Allness is *wholly* consciousness, its action is that of being totally and wholly aware. *In its timeless state of "Whole Cognition," it is wholly aware of ALL of its Infinite Self. It is aware of its every degree of progression - totally - from origin to ultimate maturity.*

It is important that we realize what is involved in the fact that this original state of infinite awareness is timeless. Timeless awareness is not limited in any way in the direction or extent of its knowing. Unhampered by any restrictions whatsoever, it is perpetually "open" to all - totally all-knowing of Self in every respect. (It is even aware of its total experience potential in the time and space positionings we call relativity.)

Because the original state of The Infinite is a condition of timelessness, all is known, *but it is all known at once.* It is like hearing all of a song instantaneously - all at once. The differentiation of each note would thus be impossible. Each note would be known - but not tangibly placed nor understood. Such is the condition of the timeless, all-knowing state of Consciousness. However, it is just this condition that allows for the innate realization of all the potentials of The Infinite to be realized, from origin to ultimate maturity. Thus the "end-product" of The Infinite, fully matured, is a reality of consciousness. However, it is an abstract fulfillment not yet consummated as a *tangible* state. This "end-product realization" permeates all being, and is the force that urges all progression towards its fulfillment.

Although the action of evolution is fully described in the previous chapter, we shall recapitulate just a bit on it. Abstractly, the mature tree resides in the seed. Its influence permeates the seed, urging and guiding it into tangible maturity. Just so the Infinite "end product," like a "ghost of wholeness," is urging and guiding The Infinite towards tangible maturity. This "ghost of wholeness" is the innate essence that permeates all, and is guiding all progression. (As implied, the "end product" includes within it, all the intermediate steps leading up to its intended maturity, as well as the realization of the matured Whole, itself.)

It is evident then, that the action that unifies every step in the universe together meaningfully and keeps it going in the right direction, is the awareness that is the "end product - The Ghost of Wholeness," which also includes the intent to *tangibly* consummate that fully known realization of Self. This grand realization is all-powerful because the certainty of a unified oneness and its direction is already established as a reality. (It knows where its going and that it can get there, since it is already there in the abstract!) *This is a realized certainty.* It is this certainty-realization that is perpetually urging and compelling all towards a greater and greater *tangible* realization of what Self is, constantly exercising its subtle guidance towards ultimate and certain fulfillment and betterment.

It is easy to see why many intuitively refer to the force of certainty-realization as Faith, though they may not understand it. Some refer to it as "The Force." Others refer to it as Love. (Christ probably understood all of this if his scriptural quotation, "God is Love" is correctly interpreted.)

The Infinite certainty-realization is the basic force of consciousness that not only knows all, but includes the intent and guidance for its realization, *tangibly.* It is the all-permeating drive for total Self-realization - the drive for the continual betterment of all. *The Certainty-realization of Infinite Cognition, is the essence of all action.*

Humanly, some have named the basic drive for continual increase and betterment of Self, "sex." This is understandable in view of the fact that the promulgation and betterment of all species is involved with sex activity in one way or another.

To recapitulate a bit more, "The realization of Infinite Self, *tangibly consummated*," is not a light statement. Yet the abstract realization of this, including the intent of its fulfillment, is the basic essence that permeates all being. Tangible fulfillment is the cognized goal of all progression, a unifying realization that is subtly guiding us all towards certain maturity. There is no force to oppose it. Call it Love, Faith or Infinite Certainty-Realization, it is the essence of all action.

All action is involved in the attainment of total Self-realization. "Re-cognition," the action of identifying the original cognition in terms of time and space is another basic activity. Self cognition and Self re-cognition will be thoroughly addressed in chapters to come.

Humankind throughout the ages has always harbored the innate realization of an overall control-of-all, but as an abstraction. It is this abstraction that has generated the idea of God, although, as we well know, the God idea has been expressed in various ways and with many forms. The full scope of exactly what God is, and how we fit into the picture is within our present understanding, but we must first release some of our old concepts rather than try to fit new concepts into the old ones. Those who are ready to grow will be flexible enough to study new ideas sincerely.

Having journeyed through these first preliminary chapters, we are perhaps ready to become better acquainted with our true Self. Let us proceed to our next chapter, "The Infinite" and perhaps fathom the grandness of the being that we truly are.

SECTOR VI

THE INFINITE

A GRATEFULNESS

Every day, I must express
my perpetual gratefulness,
for Love and Truth, and choice that's clear -
for joy, and gladness, and good cheer.

And every moment of my life -
even if it holds some strife -
finds a way to let me know,
that problems help each one to grow.

It's up to me to run my mind -
to take control of what I find,
and let no other be my voice,
by robbing me of my own choice.

It's a loving quest for me
to try to solve the mystery
of my presence in this world -
to associate with boys and girls,

and grown-ups (some so set in mind),
and animals of every kind.
What more is it I could ask,
than to face the pleasing task

of opening the door of mind
to explorations we may find,
could touch us all in Love and Truth,
and enrich the searching mind of youth? - -

Yes, I am grateful I am here -
right here, right now, and in good cheer,
and grateful for my destiny
of sharing with humanity

the issues that can help us show
each other new ways we can grow -
free, from old chains of tradition
and gaining for us the admission

to a reign of self that's far above
the lesser life we've learned to love.
I'm grateful there's a way to see
the issues of Infinity.

"IN A NUTSHELL"

To explain to someone about "The Infinite" and how we fit into the picture is kind of like one drop of the ocean trying to tell the rest of the drops that they all belong to a single, unified embodiment. Much like our human situation, the drops would probably feel that they each live their own, independent life. They would probably be only abstractly aware of the larger life in which they live and move and have their being.

In the ocean, if we may continue using it as an analogy, the wetness of the Whole belongs to each drop, and yet is shared by all - a oneness. In the same manner, the volume of the Whole belongs to each drop and is shared by all - a oneness. In fact, every characteristic of the Whole belongs to each drop, yet is a common oneness, shared by all. Even the Whole-control such as temperature stabilization, ocean level, etc., is shared by each drop.

In a similar manner, we are all "drops" in the "ocean" of Infinite Consciousness. It is the only consciousness there is, since "infinite" means "all-inclusive wholeness." There is nothing else. We are the "drops" that make up that "ocean." Each of us possesses all the characteristics of the Whole just like each drop of water in our analogy does. There is no quality of the Whole that is not integral to the part. The presence of the Whole (including its every characteristic) is the essence of each part, and thereby thoroughly pervades every "drop" of the "Ocean of Infinite Consciousness," not unlike the ocean in our analogy. It is not a "father - son" type relationship, but is actually a oneness of being, since The Infinite lives as the Whole and as its parts. As we progress, it is indeed pleasing to see how logically we all fit into this equation of oneness.

It is well to realize that we are not dealing with bodies that somehow "have awareness," as our everyday observations would normally indicate. Whatever the focus, we are dealing solely with consciousness and not bodies, per-se. Since consciousness is all there is, only consciousness can be aware. Our life consists of consciousness to consciousness relationships. Simply put, "living," is the action of consciousness being aware of itself.

In the progressing action of Self-awareness, the focus of distinctions plays an important part, for only through the awareness of distinctions can tangibility be established. When tangibility is established, life becomes rich and meaningful in terms of understanding it rather than just a bland, "knowing you're alive."

When the "Ocean of Infinite Consciousness" cognized itself as a whole, the first distinction of being was unveiled: The Whole, itself. The Whole cognized itself AS a self! Self identity was established. This was a primal step in the progression of The Infinite Presence. As incredible as it may seem, each of us are actually that same original "I," that same identity! In that timeless realization, The Infinite characterized all of itself as "I." This characterization included you and me, in fact, everyone and all, since The Infinite is all-inclusive! No one can be omitted from Infinite action. In the case of infinite consciousness as well as in our ocean analogy, every quality and characteristic of The Whole is also the shared quality and characteristic of the parts. Just as "whole-ocean wetness" is the same wetness as "drop-wetness," the "I" identity of the Whole is the same for both part and Whole.

When an individual says, "I," that person is not referring to a part or fraction of his (or her) identity, but is referring to the Whole-of-Self, even though the Whole-of-Self may not be understood for what it really is. There is no such a thing as a "half-self" or a "fractional-self." Simply put, Self requires wholeness. It is of extreme importance that we realize that there can be only one Self - one "I" identity, for there is only one Whole - one All!

The all-inclusiveness of Infinite action does not allow it to partition itself into sectors that would exclude other parts or portions, no more than the ocean can permanently split itself away from portions of itself. The Infinite is totally in contact with All, perpetually - a single, unified presence.

How we fit into a structure of only one identity is indeed a fascinating presentation, but requires a re-examination of our concepts in view of what is presented here. In our past, how many *basic* concepts have we adopted as true, that are actually questionable? Is that which we have accepted as true, really true? Our honesty is indeed, being challenged.

As we advance in our studies, we will come to realize that Infinite Consciousness cannot possibly be added to, since it is all the consciousness there is. There is no way to add to "The All." This means then that The Infinite contains its own progression.

For the action of progression to proceed, the primal "seed" must include the realization of its mature "end product," as well as all the steps leading thereto. This has been fully explained in our chapter, "Evolution." From this, we can see why every step of The Infinite's progression is already established in the Infinite Consciousness. This wholly complete, abstract realization of The Infinite Self, is totally shared with every degree of consciousness, and abides within it as its very essence. The Infinite is not blindly advancing forward, but actually knows where its going, abstract though that guidance may seem to be.

If we may say it once again, we all live and move and have our being in and as, the infinite "ocean" of consciousness. This "ocean" is not a consciousness of random actions, but is a controlled, unified activity with a definite purpose.

Regardless of the degree of understanding of Self we now have, each of us is progressing towards a more and ever more, meaningful realization of the one Infinite Presence that is our essence.

"And so, my son,

You may suspect that some books are written for the thinker alone, and not for the trifler. This is not true, for the curiosity of the trifler is actually his (or her) innate love of honesty, sniffing at that which draws the entity into a web of enchantment - an enchantment that eventually results in the fruition of the higher self within. Even the thinker may merely be satisfying a selfish motive for the moment; however, that energy of selfishness will eventually mature too, into the altruism of a realized oneness of being.

My son, each spider's web is designed to catch in it, exactly the size of insect it can handle. Are we of an inferior design? Do you not think that we too, catch in our webs, exactly what each of us is capable of handling? Is not our importance at least equal to that of a spider?"

--from the writings of Athanasios

CHAPTER VI

THE INFINITE

As we approach this subject let us walk nimbly, for "The Truth that will set us free from ignorance" has its cornerstone laid in the understanding of The Infinite. The question of our real identity and the purpose of our presence has undoubtedly been a mystery to every thinking person. It is this chapter that opens the door to the solving of this enigma, though we must proceed into chapters that follow to gain the full comprehension of who and what we are, and why we are here.

Chapter III has shown us that the essence of all that is, is purely consciousness. There is no other substance. The understanding of "The Infinite Presence" as the ALL of consciousness, abiding as one, unified Whole - the sole presence that constitutes and controls all, wholly in attendance everywhere and equally present throughout part and Whole - here, now and always - is what we are trying to tangibly present.[3]

We hesitate to use the word "God" to portray The Infinite, yet it may be the best analogy we have to offer. The common idea of God, is that "God is the creator and controlling force from which all emanated, and is therefore the source of all that is." This idea, to some extent, expresses what The Infinite is, and is the reason why we are using the name "God," temporarily. What we may have failed to fully realize is that if God created everything, then everything was created from "*his*" substance, since there was nothing else to create from! This has far-reaching implications for this means that if God is of an *infinite* nature, then "his" substance could not be of a *finite* nature. Since God is infinite, then whatever God created must also be of an infinite nature! (It is self evident, that it is impossible for something to create from itself, something that is *essentially* unlike itself.)

When we understand the full meaning of "infinite" we will see how and why God and all of us, are one single entity. We will see that each "part" of the Infinite includes the "Whole" of the Infinite, just as the drops that constitute the ocean are both the part and the whole.

---

[3] *Because the study of The Infinite borders on the abstract, a more than usual amount of repetition has been resorted to, in order to clarify and emphasize fundamental issues.*

As a rule, most dictionaries give a fair definition of "infinite," such as: [*immeasurably great - unbounded or unlimited - inexhaustible - not finite - the Infinite or the Infinite Being, God.*] How many of us are aware of the tremendous message implied by that last description: "*the Infinite Being, God*"? If just one being is "infinite," this means that: "*that one being is all inclusive* - ALL that there is." There can be no other being! Everything that is, would have to be part of that being, since an infinite Being must be wholly everywhere in its presence and control. If it was not, it would not be infinite! Its presence and whole-control would include all, including you and me. Verily, it is time to give "The Infinite" the thorough examination it truly deserves.

Christ was quoted as saying: "I and the Father are one." If this is a true quotation, Christ understood the truth about his infinite origin. Notice that Christ didn't say, "I, Jesus Christ, and the Father are one." He said, "I." The "I" that Christ is and the "I" that the Father is are one. Christ apparently understood that there is only one "I." If he had been quoted as saying, "Each of us and the Father are one," perhaps each of us would have *seriously* accepted the challenge of solving who and what we really are. We would realize that, if "The Father and I are one," then to find out "who and what I am," we must solve the problem of exactly who and what The Father is! We would realize that a full understanding of The Infinite must be gained.

We were probably all born into a somewhat careless use of the language we use. For example, if we were to ask a dozen of our friends what the difference is between "infinite" and "eternal," we would probably get a dozen different answers. Most of us have used the two words synonymously. However, the knowing of the specific difference between the two is an issue that is vital to the understanding we are trying to gain. First, let us examine the issues regarding the meaning of "eternal."

You may have read statements like, "For time and all eternity," or, "Our love will last throughout all eternity," or, "Eternally yours." These all demonstrate how the meaning of the word, "eternal," is based upon "time" as the basis of its reality. "To be, eternally," means to endure throughout all time. If there was no such a thing as time, the word "eternal" would not be in our vocabulary! The difference between the two then, is that The Eternal is based upon time as its reality and The Infinite is not. The Infinite is the all-inclusive presence which includes all time.

With time as its essential basis then, "eternal" is easily explained, since the meaning of "eternal," depends upon time. However, The Infinite is not so readily explainable. How do we go about illustrating that which includes not only everything that the meaning of life entails, but contains all Life itself, in fact, IS all life itself?

Life? Shakespeare is credited with the quote, "To be or not to be." The consciousness we have named, "Life," is the force, "to be." Regardless of how we define this force, it is apparent that all that *is*, in order "to be," must "get here" through the "door of BE-ing (Life)" or it could have no *be*-ing. It certainly could not enter through a "door of death." The force "to be" is the synthesizing consciousness - the control through which all focus and its presentation is achieved.

The idea "to be or not to be" is responsible for the concept that there is a creator. As an example, if there was nothingness, we would not even think of such a thing as a creator. However, since there is at least one apparent creation, we automatically conclude that some type of intelligence, somehow "created" it. For something "to be," means that intelligent control brought about its being and is also sustaining its presence.

The intelligent control we are referring to, is The Infinite. Although the idea of a "personal God" may be questionable to most of us, the idea of "one source through which all presence is established and controlled," is correct. This source is not mechanical in its action. It is Infinite Consciousness, including in its controlling awareness, the dominion of Self that governs its orderly progression.

We commonly describe God as "infinite," but not as "The Infinite." Most of us are probably reluctant to use "Life", or "The Infinite" as the identity of God, because of the impersonal nature such a title infers. Undoubtedly we have been influenced by our past conditioning to entertain a feeling of guilt or perhaps even sacrilegious contempt for any reference to God that might imply anything other than a human type identity. Yet, according to the Christian scriptures, even Christ referred to God as "Love." The idea of a type of "superhuman gentleman" sitting on a throne with a judgement book in his hand is definitely questionable.

Probably the most important thing we could realize about an Infinite Presence is that it is "*totally unrestricted - throughout its wholeness*." "To be, infinitely," means "to infinitely be" - as ALL - a *totality* of presence throughout all. This means, that The Infinite is *wholly* everywhere, throughout all of its Self. Like the ocean, it is wholly in attendance wherever its every drop is. It is wholly attendant to its every condition. What one part feels then, the whole of it must also feel. If one part of it could be affected by sickness, the whole of it would be so afflicted. If one tiny speck of it died, the whole of it would die. If one speck of it was imperfect in any way, then the whole must be imperfect. If one part was ignorant, then the whole must forever remain in ignorance. It was probably with this realization in mind that some early writers depicted God as "perfection." They realized that perfection is the only state of consciousness that could sustain itself as an infinite presence. Perfection is the natural state of The Infinite.

To recapitulate a bit, The Infinite Presence is simply, "The ALL." It is The Whole, all-inclusive. There is nothing else for there is only one Whole. There can be but one ALL. Being the all-inclusive presence, The Infinite includes all time - past, present and future - and therefore *includes* The Eternal.[4]

Being totally unrestricted, The Infinite then is not just partially present, but is wholly everywhere, "here and now." Not realizing this, most of us have assumed that there is us and The Infinite, and, like the drop in the ocean analogy, we find it hard to see ourself as the one, unified Whole. We habitually think in terms of the drop rather than the ocean. "There is no spot where God is not," is a commonly used religious cliche. It would be more correct to say, "There is no spot where *all* of God is not."

Let us not make the mistake of believing that The Infinite is somehow "housed in the universe." Nor is it accurate to say that the universe is "housed in The Infinite," for they are not two separate things. Like the ocean and the drop, The Infinite is both "house" and "occupant."

Due to a lack of clear understanding, we have been exposed to various, limiting ideas regarding The Infinite. Mathematically, we will hear statements like, "This goes on into Infinity," perhaps implying that The Infinite is somewhere other than where we now

---

[4] *We may wish to refer to our "Nutshell" introduction to this chapter, illustrating how an all-inclusive presence, functions as both Whole and parts - a unified oneness of being.*

are. If The Infinite could be anyplace other than everywhere, it would not be infinite.

Some might argue that The Infinite was "created," intimating that The Infinite is a type of embodiment "manufactured" by an outside power, like a toy created for the amusement of its creator. This postulate is unreasonable. Common-sense reasoning tells us that the Whole *must* contain all or it is not whole. There can be no "outside," therefore there is no "outside" power. If The Infinite contains ALL, there can be no Infinite AND something else. The Infinite is therefore completely independent of any basis other than itself. It is the one and only sovereign presence. *There is no other being*.

Thus far, we are becoming better acquainted with some of the concepts that describe The Infinite. We also have taken a look at some commonly accepted ideas that may have confused us. At the risk of "spreading ourselves out too thin," we will continue to air out related issues. Although it may seem that we are "dancing with philosophy," it is essential that we cover every approach we can think of. Hopefully the synopsis which follows, will tie up the loose ends.

At this point, it may be wise for us to reconsider this question: Which came first - Consciousness or God? Now, if Consciousness was first, then it created God. Being first, it would have to be the primal creator. Yet, if God came first and created consciousness, how could God originally function without consciousness? Which then was first?

This sounds a lot like, "Which came first, the chicken or the egg?" The answer is that both of them had to originally be "there." The egg was there, but inside the egg the mature chicken also resided, much as the manner in which the seed of a tree holds the abstract wholeness of the fully developed tree. In every fertile egg or seed is the abstract realization of the "end product." The "end product" is the abstract blueprint of wholeness that guides every progression towards its eventual fulfillment.[5]

If there is one thing to be understood about life, it is that it has to be a progression since it obviously is not retrogressing back "into the seed," nor is it the stillness essential to a "death-state." Most of us can accept as self-evident that life is not death nor a retrogression. This leaves no other alternative except that The Infinite now is, and always has been, progressing. In this light we can view it as a giant seed, progressing towards its maturity, similar to the action of a tree seed or any other type seed. In fact, "The Infinite Seed" in this respect, is no different than any other seed. It too, contains the "end product" of its progression.

The "end product" of The Infinite obviously is quite an order. One might ask, "How can this be - an end product of The Infinite?" To explain this, we must remember that consciousness is an action. Its action is "being aware." Since it is timeless in its primal action of cognition,[6] it is continuously aware of every aspect of its infinite Self, "beginning" to "end," for there is nothing that can block or deny

---

[5] *See Chapter IV "Evolution."*

[6] *Time as a function of re-cognition is explained in a chapter to follow.*

a timeless realization. Like the "tree in the seed," the realization is not tangible except in abstract terms. In abstract terms, the timeless realization is "all-knowing" and "all-understanding" of all that can possibly be known and understood. Every potential, including the full *relative* comprehension of The Infinite Self, is abstractly embraced and is the basic essence of all self-awareness. In a sense we could call this abstract realization, our divine DNA - inherent in all.

The "end product" in its abstract realization of The Infinite as a "matured-Self," includes the certainty-realization of: "*Its possible, since its already done.*" This is the "*I am - I can - I do*" impetus that is subtly directing Infinite progression forward. As mentioned before, it is very probable that this abstract "end-product realization" is the "Holy Ghost" of Biblical lore. A more fitting description would be something like "The Awareness of Wholeness" or "The Whole Ghost."

We must not lose sight of the fact that The Infinite is not a body of some type that somehow moves around and acts. The Infinite is the action, itself. It is purely, action. It identifies its Self through the use of forms and formations (bodies). It is a situation wherein "awareness has a body" (or bodies as we may wish to phrase it), and not one wherein "bodies have awareness." Contrary to general appearances, all bodies are "consciousness-formations." All that is, is structured by and from The Infinite Consciousness, which essentially constitutes every bit and parcel of presence that there is. There is nothing that is not a formation of The Infinite Presence. The mechanics of this formative action are elaborated on in our coming chapters. (We may feel that we are an awareness independent of the all-permeating God-presence we are describing, but there is no denying that there can be no other presence. Perhaps we can relate again, to "the ocean and the drops" to reconfirm the credibility of this important realization of oneness.)

As we are beginning to see, The Infinite is more than just a dimension of life. It IS all life. In the interest of clearing away more debris and perhaps opening a few more doors, we will examine other related issues, as well as the credibility of there being only one life-force.

For instance, "Why does life *have* to be infinite?" Why couldn't it be finite? To answer this, we must explore the idea of "a beginning of life." By definition, anything that is of a finite nature must have a beginning and an end to it. If we can see that Life has no boundaries, we will see that it *has* to be infinite.

If "life-activity" is the essence of *all*, our reasoning shows us that life could never have had a beginning. Why? First of all, let us recall that it is absolutely impossible to get "somethingness" from an *absolute* "nothingness." Secondly, we must agree that life is action, as opposed to a death type, stillness. (We must realize that if activity was not always the fact - a condition of perpetual presence - it would be impossible to "manufacture" it out of nothingness or a total stillness of some kind.) As an example, let us imagine a scenario where all was at a dead stop - everything! What then could there ever be to "start things moving," and initiate a beginning? A "death-force?" "Death" is a condition of total stillness! Neither stillness nor "nothingness" can "start something up" so it can "have a beginning." It is obvious that if life-activity was not always a reality, then an eternal stillness would prevail forever, since activity could never be initiated by "non-activity."

In order to clarify this issue a bit more, let's suppose for the moment that a non-life force somehow was a presence - a type of "non-integration" force. A non-life force, were this somehow possible, could have no functional activity except possibly "dis-integration," a force of annihilation. This possibility is ludicrous, *since if there was such a force, it could not allow itself any being either, and would disintegrate itself*. Our reasoning thus assures us that all presence has to come through the activity of a Life essence. It is apparent then, that if Life could not have been generated by a stillness, or "force of non-activity", then Life always was. The initial life activity is and always was, a perpetual, self-sustaining presence. There never was such a thing as "a beginning" for if Life was ever stopped there would be nothing living to give it a "beginning."

Recapitulating then, we can see that the Life-force could never have had a "beginning." Secondly, it is the *only* force, since without it there could be no "BE-ing" - no focus - no integration - no presence, whatsoever. Life then is not only sovereign, but boundless in its every aspect - in every "direction," for there could be no being - no action whatsoever - that was not under its auspices. This means there could be no force or boundaries of any nature that could conflict with its all-inclusiveness. It therefore, is infinite. It is the sovereign, unbounded Infinite Presence - "The Infinite."

It may be well for us to emphasize that the possibility of two or more "Infinites" is an impossibility. The Infinite has been shown to be all-inclusive, since it can have no fences. There cannot be two "all-inclusives" since one must contain the other or vice versa. There can be but one Whole - one Infinite.

And now that we have so extensively examined The Infinite, we are better prepared to learn how it is the God we have been so earnestly seeking. We are prepared to see how The Infinite, from an original, timeless stature, had to establish a state of time and place in order to understand itself. We are prepared to see how we figure into this overall progression of "The Infinite."

SYNOPSIS of CHAPTER VI

1. It is obvious there can only be one Whole (one "All There Is").

2. "The Infinite" is the name given to "All There Is." It is an infinity of consciousness.

3. The original state of The Infinite is a state of timelessness. Consciousness is the action of "being aware," and because it is originally, timelessly aware, it is all-knowing. It is omniscient. There is nothing hidden to it. It is important that we realize that the timeless state of all-knowingness is never "erased," but is the perpetual "perfection-reality" from which all emanates.

4. The unified awareness that is The Whole, is not a random activity, but is an organized and progressing presence. It is tangibly establishing itself in terms of a greater and greater Self-realization. This progression is innately directed and impelled by the inner realization of its ultimate "end-product." (This action is not unlike the action of a tree seed, wherein the consciousness of the "end product," like a "ghost of wholeness," permeates the entire seed, subtly controlling and guiding it as it develops into maturity.)

5. The Infinite, as well as being "The Controlling <u>Whole</u>," is also the integral essence and control of each and every part! All action, including our presence, IS the action of The Whole.

6. Our essence is The Whole, itself. As we can see, the Biblical quotation, "The Father and I are one," is truly worthy of consideration.

7. The infinite, unbounded nature of The Whole, insures that every quality of The Infinite Consciousness is shared with every degree of its presence. Each "part" of The Infinite Whole, equally shares all the qualities of the Whole, much as the drops in the ocean share the qualities of the whole ocean. <u>Infinite nature allows no boundaries within or without</u>. "There is no spot where <u>all</u> of God is not."

8. The action we call "life" is actually The Infinite, functioning. It is the integrating intelligence - the action through which, ALL is being presented in terms of distinctions and thus tangibly understood. The Infinite does not "possess" life, it *is* life. Since all life is a progression, The Infinite is in a state of perpetual progression.

9. Living is the action of consciousness being aware of itself.

10. Because The Infinite is <u>*the*</u> life force, it is the only integrating force. Therefore, all that is, must arrive through its auspices. This means that there can be no presence in opposition to The Infinite. It is therefore, omnipotent - the one and only power - the almighty presence.

11. Any disruption of the Infinite force "to be" would automatically erase all presence. Since The Infinite is the only presence and without external or <u>internal</u> boundaries, it is <u>wholly</u>

affected if any part of it is affected. If it were to be "touched" by any imperfection, the whole of it would be nullified. This means that it always has been and continually abides in, a state of perfection.

As we can see, the properties involved in "being infinite" are far reaching. When we say, "God is infinite," few, if any of us, realize how far the "Infinite arm" reaches. One, all-inclusive presence is not easy to swallow as a fact - not when we view the seemingly independent actions of ourselves and those about us, not to mention other realms such as the animal and the insect species.

Understandably, our discourse regarding The Infinite is extensive, and regrettably a bit repetitious, to say the least. Our next two chapters deal with the factors regarding our personal presence, and "how it got 'here'."

WHOLLY ONE

Mother and father act as the beast
whose throbbing message of the groin,
brings satisfaction at the least -
and maybe entry, through their loins.

Does animal kingdom reign supreme,
to bring forth the nights and days,
or is God the ruling King
who controls, and calls the plays?

Who decided you'd be born,
and as animal-man attain
a presence in the earthy reign
and at the mercy of a brain -

a brain born with pattern etched
in DNA, to "pave the way" -
a beast that's born to belly hunger,
born to sexually, "make its play?"

To realize God, we go through beast
and the Self within's, the key?
We suffer through the earthly life
to find our true identity?

Our vision focusses on love,
for what we love, is what we deem
important to retain in sight -
important to our self-esteem.

We see with the eyes of an animal
a world of jumbled wants and fears -
some that tend to make us fall -
yet we develop, through the years - -

Could there be more than meets the eye
and the Truth yet hides, in Time?
Could "the animal" be a lie,
and an experience, sublime -

to unfold all, that we can be
and are waiting to become -
to prepare us all to see,
that we all, are wholly, One?

Our life, through "manly-animal,"
confusing as it all may seem -
will know God as "One - The All"
though for now, it seems a dream.

SECTOR VII

COGNITION (THE INVISIBLE "I AM" PRESENCE)

THE INFINITE "I"

It is "I" that claims us all;
all one "I," one "I" in all.
Why is it so hard to see
the "I," our sole identity?

What could live and what could "die,"
if its essence was not "I,"
in fact, what is it we could be
if "I" did not claim you and me?

And what controls before the womb,
during life and beyond the tomb?
In whose domain, does all Truth lie,
if not the living presence, "I?"

And, if so, must matter be
of the "I" comprising you and me?
Does all "being" then rely
on one, all-inclusive "I?"

The day will come when you will find
the question weighing on your mind -
tugging, forcing you to try
to solve the Truth, regarding "I.

"And so, my son,

You quote to me from your religious passages about 'The all-knowing God.' And is not God all-knowingness, a timeless 'now-realization' of all that is, all that was, and all that is going to be? Therefore would you not say that God needs not 'wait around' to learn through time, for 'He' already knows it all now?

And you, my son, if you knew a song, and it was all played 'now' (instantaneously), do you think you would recognize the tune, or would the notes all playing at once confuse you? Would you not require that which we call 'time' in order to tangibly appreciate each note? It is so, with God also, my son. There is a reason for our time experience. It is through the process of re-cognition that the meaning and significance of each factor of Self becomes tangibly expressed and appreciated.

Yet, let us be ever aware, my son, that the timeless, all-knowingness is of vital importance to us, for it is the basic awareness of all. It is the infinite reservoir - all awareness, in its virginal state of perfection. It is our essence. It is this essence that nourishes and guides us, as we journey through our time experiences. May we ever become more awake to its voice."

--from the writings of Athanasios

CHAPTER VII

COGNITION (THE INTANGIBLE "I AM" PRESENCE)

Our last chapter served to give us some idea of how involved the idea of "The All" can be. We were introduced to many factors regarding the "what," and some of the factors regarding the "how," but the "who" is left to the reader's imagination for the time being. We are slowly working our way towards the the full meaning of "Who," but require a bit more groundwork in order to present that understanding, tangibly. We have appropriately named "The All," "The Infinite," presenting it as a unified, living presence - "The Infinite I." However, there is still more to be understood about how it operates and how this applies to us.

As illustrated in Chapter III, consciousness is all there is, for there is nothing else, yet it is obvious that in order for the variations of life around us to exist, there must be variations of one sort or another in consciousness. This chapter is primarily concerned with the presentation of The Infinite in its intangible, timeless state: "the State of Cognition."

Most of us take our "identity-sense" of "I," and "I am" for granted, never suspecting that those realizations, were steps in the primal progression of The Infinite. (It is evident they just didn't appear out of a nothingness.) The original "'I AM' Cognition" was the step that opened the door to the tangible focus of distinctions that we now experience.

"Cognition" is really not as complicated as it sounds. It really means, "knowing." We have chosen the word "cognition" because it is related to the word "re-cognition" which is a type of secondary "look" or "knowing" of that which is already known. (Our next chapter focusses upon re-cognition.)

Cognition is explained in general terms but we are also presenting its specific progression into the state of: "the knowing of Self, in terms of a 'who' - in terms of 'I AM'." This step by step progression is of no small import since The Whole, in its every degree of enlightenment, includes its every part. Each progression of The Infinite Consciousness, totally and thoroughly involves ALL of it. This includes us, for as every quality of water is included in its every drop, just so, every quality of The Progressing Whole, is assimilated by us. For The Infinite to realize anything at all, means that *all* consciousness is included in that realization.

When The Infinite came to the realization of its Self as an identity (a "who"), every degree of its consciousness was included in that Self-Identity realization. In a sense, we could say that we were all "born" into identity status at that precise instant for this was the point at which "I AM" self-identity in terms of a "who," was achieved for all being. The idea that "each of us has a soul" is perhaps substantiated, if our "soul" is defined as the perfect identity presence just described. (Some would call this "our spiritual presence.")

All consciousness - Whole and parts - was thus endowed with the realization of Self-identity, although, at this point, it was established in the abstract state of timelessness. The next step of progression, re-cognition, would bring it into the state of tangible realization.

And now, let us look at our outline of the step by step progression of the Infinite Cognition-Consciousness as it evolved into the "I AM," status we have just described.

THE PROGRESSION OF COGNITION INTO THE REALIZATION OF "I AM."

Presented in the preceding chapter is the fact that The Infinite is Life, and therefore always has been and always will be progressing. The Infinite, as a Whole and as a part, always has been and is, proceeding towards its ultimate goal of total Self-realization in terms of *tangible* self-understanding and presence. As has been indicated, it is not progressing in a random, haphazard fashion, but in a pattern of overall unity that is "centrally" controlled.[7]

The steps of the progress of The Infinite Cognition can be likened to the development action in a fertilized chicken egg. Just as the *abstract* chicken resides in the undeveloped egg, there is a complete, and wholly fulfilled, *abstract*, Infinite-Self, inhabiting The Infinite. This abstract Self is the entirety of The Infinite, realized as its every degree of development, even unto and including its tangibly mature state. Just as the abstract chicken in the undeveloped egg impels and guides all activity towards eventual maturity, the abstract presence of The Infinite Self is impelling and guiding itself towards its ultimate goal.[8] *Like The Infinite Self, a chicken, during the period its formation is transpiring, has no tangible structure called "I."* However, once the formation of the chicken is completed, the identity of the chicken is viably established, and no longer is an obscurity. Though the chicken at that point, is still in the egg and in darkness, it is aware of what has transpired: The whole of its self is now consummated as a complete and organized identity - a viable presence. And now, as a viable identity, the chicken arrives at the

---

[7] *Please refer to Chapter II to review this all-important issue.*

[8] *Please refer to Chapter IV.*

realization, "I AM," and thus evolves to the awareness of itself AS an identity - a "who." This realization, although abstract, is valid, but since it is abstract, it is consummated in terms of feeling, rather than in the terms of "outer perception" such as we are normally accustomed to. To identify itself *tangibly*, the chicken must break the shell of the egg, which of course, is its next step.

The Infinite Cognition progressed in a manner similar to that of the chicken in the egg. It too, organized itself in its "egg" (its all-knowing state of Infinite Consciousness). In steps similar to the chicken forming in the egg, it evolved itself into identity status: the abstract realization of itself as an identity, (a "who"). And thus, with viable identity established, The Infinite arrived at the realization, "I AM!" Now when The Infinite did arrive at this point of Self-identity, the maturity of its timeless state was consummated. (Like the mature chick breaking out of its shell, its next step, re-cognition, would carry The Infinite, and thus, us, into the realm of tangibility.)

Each of us, as a part of The Infinite, was thus established as what may be called a spiritual identity: the abstract realization "I AM." The perfect "I AM" presence that is the essence of us, in fact, ALL, had been realized. (Again, this set the stage for tangible Self-realization, the next step of Infinite progression. In our next chapter we will address the tangible birth of all Self-identity.)[9]

----

[9] *Our analogy has shown us how Infinite Cognition, like the chicken in the egg, goes through the steps of reaching full maturity, thereby establishing Self as a viable identity. However this is not entirely correct, for in the case of The Infinite, the development portrayed is actually timeless. We have introduced time into its portrayal for purposes of clarity. In a timeless state, The Infinite is all "there" - wholly in attendance, simultaneously - from "beginning," through all its intermediate stages, to the "end."*

As previously mentioned, Infinite awareness has no boundaries, within or without. Thus, The Infinite Cognition, "I AM" is our primal awareness, in fact, the primal awareness of all that is. This primal awareness did not "shut down" at maturity. (We must not lose sight of the fact that it is timeless. Therefore, it is ever, our ever-present, basic essence that we continuously draw from.)[10] As we progress, we will find that this divine presence, our true essence and basic awareness, will become more of a <u>tangible</u> reality to us.

It is not of any small significance for us to realize that while the chicken was in the egg, there was no extraneous data introduced. If the original substance the chicken was comprised of was absolutely pure, it stands to reason that the chicken was formed in absolute purity. Just so, The Infinite houses no error, for the Truth is all that there actually is to it (a lie is something that is not). The Infinite in its timeless, "I AM" state, <u>*still is, and remains forever, the pristine purity of timeless being - the perfect presence, that is ever with us, in fact, is us, as we will come to understand*</u>. [The fact that we make mistakes in mathematics does not change the pristine correctness of that which we made mistakes <u>about</u>. In like manner, no matter how we identify our original essence (The timeless "I AM" realization), no matter what mistakes we make, it too, remains ever and forever the pristine perfection it is, and always was.]

To elaborate a bit more, The Infinite Cognition is not a perception of seeing as we commonly interpret it, but is the pure feeling, "I AM" - it is the genuine and original awareness of The

---

[10] *The Infinite identity, "I AM," does not stop just because it is being re-cognized in the time-place frame we have named, "The relative universe." It is an ever-present, all-pervading, timeless constancy. Intuitively, some have named it "our Soul." In reality, it <u>is</u> our Self in our abstract state of perfection.*

Infinite Self, be-ing. In this timeless realization, it feels its Self ("I AM") for what it is: Infinite "isness" - a unified oneness - Whole and parts "beginning to end," as the one omnipresent, omnipotent and omniscient identity, in its every aspect of realization. This ever-present constancy of intangible presence is the same abstract "I" we each, more or less, claim as our own "I," and IS the reality of the Self we are. It is our basic "Self-feeling." It is so commonplace and natural to us that we are probably unaware of it, tangibly. This realization is not a condition of perceiving "second hand" information like we are used to receiving, based on our outer perceptions. Nor can it be described as "inner realization," since "inner" implies "outer." It is genuine - the original. It is "first hand." It is the positive, all-knowing realization "I AM," wholly constituting all that is. Without this reality of focussed, "isness awareness," the next step of progression would be impossible.

The Cognition state of The Infinite then is not the ultimate of progression. It can be likened to a situation where we are hearing all the notes of a song simultaneously, thereby leaving us void when it comes to understanding what we are perceiving. The Infinite Cognition is consciousness that has not yet been processed into tangibility. It is the primary state of The Infinite, and although it has its drawbacks, it is because of its unrestricted nature of timelessness, that the infinite presence of Cognition can be wholly and completely everywhere, similar to the way the whole of the ocean is always present throughout its entirety. As an ever-present reservoir of all-knowingness, the infinite cognition is always, *wholly* in attendance as every aspect of its Self. It is an ever-present constancy. Every degree of life, shares this reservoir of all-knowingness.

Infinite Cognition then is the Infinite, "I AM" realization - the timeless, all-pervading ever-presence, from which all proceeds.[11]

Some of the scientists of an earlier age, theoretically depicted an all-inclusive, ethereal presence in which all is housed and proceeds from, and named it "The Ether." They described it as the basic, all-inclusive presence in which all inheres - totally invisible, undetectable, and ever-present. Even some of the modern day schools of thought accept "The Ether" as a reality, realizing that "somethingness" could never inhere from a nothingness. Our following chapter explains how this "ether" - "the infinite ocean of 'I AM' Cognition," progressed into the life we are now experiencing.

The original realization of Cognition ("I AM") is not a small step in progression. Again, we must be aware that this first, abstract "I AM" realization of The Infinite is totally composed of feeling, and is not the analytic type perception we are so commonly used to, such as seeing and comparing. The timeless realization, "I AM," is the virginal cognition of <u>Self-Identity</u> from which all awareness proceeds. It is our basic <u>Self</u>-cognition -- our true identity. It appropriately has been called "Spirit" by many who intuitively grasped the fact that our essence is truly divine.

---

[11] *We must be cautious not to make the mistake of thinking that the infinite "ocean" of Self-cognition is somehow confined or enclosed. (Regretfully, it was necessary to portray it as such in our analogies in order to clearly present its progression.)*

SECTOR VIII

RE-COGNITION

"And so, my son,

This presentation is perhaps one of the highest offerings we can place upon your plate, for we are striving to weave into tangibility, that which constitutes the 'power-force' control you may have named 'God.'

By now you have probably realized that life <u>*has*</u> *to be a progression. If God is life, then life is God, and so, is progressing. Because we have progressed we have no problem in looking back towards our own infancy, when we were in the baby state. What then is to prevent us from looking back and reviewing God's progression when God was just a 'baby?' Yes, my son, we* <u>*have*</u> *spoken about this before.*

We are used to dealing with everything in terms of time, my son, but in our conceiving of God in the baby state, we are focussing upon a 'before-time' era. Life includes all, even the pre-time era that progression has carried us beyond. <u>*Time was born, my son, through the womb of progressing consciousness, just as you were*</u>*. It is through the time factor that the distinctions of life become tangible to us, but we must proceed slowly if we are to digest the depth of this reality. You may suspect by now, that there is more to time than a measurement that is based upon the movements of our planet around the sun.*

And so, my son, what would conditions be like if you were living your life now <u>*without*</u> *the 'time' you are so used to? Distance would be no problem at all, since you could go from New York to Los Angeles in 'no time at all.' In fact, if time wasn't a factor, what could stop you from being in both places at once? What would stop you from being* <u>*everywhere*</u>*, all at once? You can see, my son, that* *without time, distance is meaningless. And if you are everywhere, all in the same instant, how can you say, 'This belongs here,' and, 'That should be there?' 'Here' and 'there' become meaningless do they not, since 'here' and 'there' would be everywhere? Do you see what a vital factor time is to tangibility? For something to become* understandably *distinct, my son, it must rest somewhere in the dimension we call time.*

Yes, we talked about how the distance between cities is meaningless without time, but what about the inner *distance in the objects about you? Are not all objects established in terms of 'distance-dimensions' of length, of width and of height? But without time, we have no distance! Without distance, no dimensions! Without dimensions, no objects! Without objects, no tangibility! Yes, my son, you may be a bit confused by now, for it is a far-reaching reflection to realize that the whole structure of the visible universe is based upon time and distance. If you could somehow 'erase' time and distance out of the universe, the universe would collapse into a meaningless presence - completely intangible. What could you see if there were no dimensions to 'stretch and hold' everything into formations?*

And now, my son, we are ready for another look at the 'God-baby.' You do realize by now, that the substance of all is consciousness? The 'God-baby' state is the Whole of consciousness in a state of intangibility. This Infinite Presence always was and is, our original state - an abstract awareness of all. Being abstractly aware is kind of like having a consciousness of something being all around you, but not being quite able to put your finger on it. In the 'God-baby' state, there was no awareness of tangible *distinctions although as an infinite abstractness, this awareness was wholly all pervading, in fact all-inclusive, as a unified oneness. There never was any beginning to it nor any end. You can see, my son, there was nothing to limit it in any way, for there is not now nor was there ever, anything else. This 'God-baby' is the virginal, Infinite Consciousness, that is everywhere - omnipotent, omniscient, omnipresent and 'omnicontrolling.' It is infinitely everywhere in every way. It is the 'I' that you and that everyone else is. How the 'God-baby' has progressed to the degree where it realized its 'Self' as the sovereign distinctions 'I,' and 'I am,' and how these realizations progressed into the manifested universe and its inhabitants as we perceive it today, is indeed a fascinating story. However, enough for the moment. Peace be with you, my son."*

--from the writings of Athanasios

THE REALITY OF "I"

Whether boldly or in disguise,
each day, the question will arise:
"What's my real identity -
who, or what, is really me?"

It prevails like the scent of food -
always there, like a hidden mood -
for, like the truth behind each lie,
there's a reality to "I."

The "I" of me and the "I" of you -
are they but one, or are they two?
Are apples, hanging on a tree,
all parts of the tree, or a sovereignty?

If the "I" is our family tree,
are we "I-apples," all named "me?"
Is God the "tree-I," and holding all -
and the <u>only</u> "I" - and alive as all?

Oh, how do I identify,
the Self, that seems to live and die?
Is there a new way we can try -
to get an honest look at "I?"

CHAPTER VIII

RECOGNITION

So far we have introduced two basic functions involving The Whole, both of them abstract: (1) The total realization of The Infinite from infinite "beginning" to infinite "end"[12] and (2) The all-encompassing Self-Cognition of The Infinite as the realization, "I AM."

The third basic function of The Whole is the realization, "I AM," in terms of re-cognition. It was through this action that the infinite identity, the "who" of Infinite Cognition became tangibly manifested. It was a genesis of The Whole into a state of tangible realization. This genesis included each and every one of us. In this chapter we examine the fundamentals of re-cognition and then show how this action brought about the "birth" of the universe as we now know it.

In our preceding chapter, we spoke of how The Infinite progressed into the realization of "I AM" in terms of Cognition. This showed how every degree - every component of The Infinite awareness was imbued with the realization of "selfness." Thus, every "speck" of being was imbued with the awareness "I AM," but as an abstract realization. It is indeed a bit mind-boggling to realize that everything - every drop of water, every grain of sand, every atomic particle - in fact, everything - all being, of any nature whatsoever, is

---

[12] *An end or beginning is approachable but not possible in an infinite situation. However, we have illustrated thus for purposes of clarity, in our portrayal of "the totality that includes every aspect of infinite presence."*

a specific self - an "I AM" awareness. If we liken The Infinite "I AM" to the ocean and how the ocean shares its every attribute with its every drop of water, it is easier for us to see that when The Infinite arrived at "I AM" status, all that is - every "drop" of being - shared that same individuality.

It perhaps is even more mind-boggling to realize what happened when The Infinite Wholeness achieved the realization "I AM" in terms of RE-cognition. To see what happened, we must first understand the action of re-cognition.

Re-cognition is actually a second cognition of that which is already cognized. (It is impossible to re-cognize something you have not been previously cognizant of.) It is through re-cognition that the action of "creation" transpires, for it is here that the action of "conception" takes place. When you re-cognize something, you automatically conceive it in terms of "when," and also in terms of "where," although you are not limited to these factors. Technically speaking, this is a creation of "what is," according to your re-cognition of it.

We normally think of "creation" in terms of something outside of us. However, the concept of "outside of us" is housed in our mind. We must understand that all creation is actually housed in the abode we call, "mind." Re-cognition takes place in our mind, conceiving all into terms of time and place, thus establishing it as memory-consciousness. All conception (creation) is a memory-positioning established in terms of relativity - "time and space." Through the action of memory recall, all is readily available to us, so that we can "make sense" of that which we discern. Thus, our positions of significance and meaning become comprehensible.
Logically, we have reasoned out that "somethingness" can never be established from a nothingness. This rules out the "creation" of

something new, for ALL, already IS. However, re-cognition re-establishes what IS, in the relative terms of time and space, as mentioned above. It is an evolving of the abstract realization of The Infinite into a condition wherein all is tangibly discernable.

It perhaps takes a great stretch of our imagination to fathom the magnitude of what happened when The Infinite Wholeness arrived at the point of re-cognizing its totality. This meant that The Infinite, itself was totally re-established in terms of time and place. Indeed, when The Infinite, *as an all-embracing "I AM" awareness,* re-cognized itself, it was a grand step in realization, for through this action, *The Whole, from the abstractness of Cognition, was tangibly conceived in terms of "I AM" awareness*! This "one-time," Infinite Conception, established ALL in terms of time, and in terms of space! The Infinite Wholeness - every degree of "I AM" awareness - was thus conceived into a tangible presence. The universe was born, in terms of the time and space factors essential to its tangible realization. It is kind of exciting to logically understand how this great action came about!

As is evident then, time and space are actually functions of our consciousness, and not a type of stability "out there" that can be utilized for positioning things in. There is no "out there" to an infinite level of presence. There is only infinite consciousness and its utilization. That which we call "memory," is actually the common "reservoir-of-re-cognition." It houses all of the tangible realization of being. It is in memory that all time and space exists. As we can see, memory is not a small issue for through its auspices, tangibility is possible. Otherwise, tangibility would be impossible.

And now, with this preliminary view of the structure of tangible realization, let us examine more of the factors involved in re-cognition.

To illustrate the evolving of Infinite Re-cognition, we will, once more, rely on analogies. (In our attempt to clarify this all important issue, we find again, that some repetition is necessary. We trust that sincere students will understand.)

Lets go back to the idea of an unformed chick in the egg. Until it is completely formed, the chick is not a viable identity, i.e., "a self." Even when fully formed in the egg, it is not a fully valid self until cognized as a self. A self must be acknowledged before it can act in terms of a self. The chick in the egg, when totally unified, must cognize its own, now complete, identity before it can break its way out of its shell. [Its breaking out of its shell is not a mechanical process, but one of volition, therefore, before it can do anything on its own, it must cognize itself AS a self - as an identity ("I AM!").] Only after self-realization can it act as a self, and thus break the shell, and free itself from the abstractness of "shell confinement." Then, as an entity, it proceeds to *re-cognize* itself ("I AM"), in the tangible terms of time and space. Thus the chick acknowledges its selfhood twice - first in terms of feeling, as an abstract self-presence inside the shell and then as a perceptible, tangible self-presence outside the shell. (First in terms of cognition, and then in terms of re-cognition.)

The Infinite Whole progressed in a manner very similar to that of the chick described above, for it too, had to establish identity realization twice. Its Selfhood had to be established first as an abstract identity (a "who") in the abstractness of timelessness and then as a tangible identity (a "who") in terms of time and space.

Like an unformed chick in an "egg of abstract timelessness," the force of "I-realization" brought The Infinite to the point of complete and total unification. The Whole of The Infinite was thus totally unified as a viable, though abstract identity: a single self of organized presence and it thus cognized itself AS an identity (I AM!) for the first time.[13] The Infinite then was capable of action as a self. Like the fully consummated chick in the egg it was ready to "break out of its shell" and proceed into tangible realization.[14]

With its identity thus validated, the Infinite then re-cognized itself ("I AM!"), *in terms of time and space.* Through this action of re-cognition (I AM!), it identified its own identity tangibly, thus bringing into tangibility every degree of Self as an individual "who" - an individual "I AM!" . This colossal realization was similar to the chicken breaking out of its egg shell. This action of Infinite identification (the re-cognition of its own Infinite Self) resulted in the creation of the tangible universe, *since the "chick" that was brought into tangibility in this case was The Infinite Whole, itself.*[15] We should make note that the "who" we are speaking of here, encompasses the Whole of all that is, although we have used a chick for our analogy. We are talking on an infinite level.

A common misconception is the belief that a "Creator" could somehow act, and make something out of a nothingness. This is not

---

[13] *This action was also explained in the preceding chapter.*

[14] *For purposes of clarity, we have once more resorted to presenting the timeless Cognition in terms of time.*

[15] *Strangely enough, a parallel to the action of Infinite Identity-Cognition and its Re-cognition is Biblically portrayed in the first and second chapters of Genesis, as the First Creation and The Second Creation.*

true. Creation on the level we are addressing, is the action of establishing the abstract presence of The Infinite into a tangible presence. Time and space are two of the prime essentials of this tangibility. Time and space were not just "sitting out there" to be used. They too were created through the action of the second "I AM" realization: re-cognition. When something is re-cognized, it is conceived in terms of "what, when, where, how and why," and includes, if the conception is thorough, every possible significance and relationship of that which has been re-cognized. Time and Space are thus created. That is what the action of The Infinite Creation consisted of. It was not the making of something out of nothing.

When the universe was thus conceived through The Infinite Re-cognition "I AM," it was indeed a grand and immaculate conception involving the totality of all presence.[16] In this infinite action, The Whole of The Infinite Self was conceived in exact and total perfection, and perfectly positioned in terms of both time and space, those positions relative to the significance of every degree of The Infinite. It was an instantaneous action that resulted in the tangible birth of the universe into the condition we call, "existence."[17]

We must not make the mistake of thinking that the tangible universe was born in a condition of maturity. It was actually born in

---

[16] *One might pause to ask why the first action of Self Cognition ("I AM!") did not create the tangible universe. The reason for this is that the first action was of a timeless nature. It did result in what we might call "the organization of The Whole" into Self-identity, but as an abstract presence. Only re-cognition can bring about tangibility as we know it.*

[17] *This is probably what modern science has alluded to as the "Big Bang."*

the baby state. The reason for this is that each component of The Infinite, originally is exactly equal with one another in every way. As each drop of water in the ocean shares every quality of the ocean, just so each component of The Infinite shares every quality of The Infinite, including the quality of self-volition. Each component is absolutely free to make its own choice and thus, is free to develop in its own individual manner. We are each a component of The Infinite. If we were born fully mature, we would be but robots or puppets. As it is, we are free and always have been free to determine our own expression in the manner each of us directs.

Every component of The Infinite was wholly and simultaneously born into a state of tangibility,[18] but as inconceivably small "units" of the minutest possible degree of tangible "I AM-awareness." Influenced by the same, shared essence, the development of each unit evolved into a continuously greater and greater unity of shared realization. Through this action, the realization we call "the visible universe" evolved into the vast structure of orderly consciousness it now represents.

Our primal choices were probably exercised in terms of a magnetic type affinity for one another, for at that point, we were building our primal inventory of tangible experience. As each of us developed, our progression was guided and ever will be guided, by the presence of Infinite Cognition: our basic essence. And, as the drops of the ocean are one with the whole of the ocean, just so is each component of The Infinite a unity with The Whole. The essence we all share is the same, in fact, we all are the one (and only) "I." There is no other "who."

---

[18] "Let There Be Light," may be an appropriate remark here.

Since The Whole (and thus, <u>its</u> intent) is our essence, our innate intent is one and the same, shared by all, and is directed towards the higher evolvement of The Whole, subtle as that progressive force may be to most of us. Whether we are aware of it or not, our every choice serves The Whole, regardless of our understanding or our misunderstanding of this great fact. In choosing freely, each of us establishes our own inventory of experiences, and we progress accordingly. Yet the intent of The Infinite for a total and tangible, harmonious unification, affects us all, and is the guiding force that is ever with us. The Infinite "I" is the "common denominator." It is the essence of ALL and thus ties us all together as a single unity, like a thread running through all life. Thus we are all one - The Infinite - for there is no other being. (The fact that there is but one, original "I," <u>infinite</u> in its scope, allows no other conclusion.)

We have established how the All-knowing status of Infinite Cognition permeates all in the abstract state of timelessness, in fact, is the essence of all. It is an everpresence with no boundaries. Re-cognition, however is in a continually developing state. Since both of these actions comprise our basic consciousness, some clarification is necessary, though again, we must lean on a bit of review and some repetition.

In a sense, we can say that consciousness consists of two domains. The abstract domain, of course, is that of The Infinite Cognition. The domain of re-cognition however, is the action of selection and conception into a tangible structure, a sort of "memory reservoir." In this action, conception takes place. Some conceptions are drawn from our essence, which perhaps, is the action named, "intuition." However, we also draw heavily from that which is already manifested through previous re-cognition. What may be a bit hard to grasp is that this is all taking place in consciousness. That which we call "The Universe" is not "out there." It is actually housed in Mind. Most of our readers are aware of the fact that many metaphysical schools focus on the idea that "All is mind - all is mental." Perhaps this idea could be better expressed by saying that "Mind consists of all that has been conceived through re-cognition."

In this text, we shall classify all re-cognition as "the mental realm" or if one prefers, "Mind." "Mind" includes memory. Memory is "the reservoir of all re-cognition," but not the boundary of it. It holds all re-cognized significance and meaning. It is continually expanding as progression takes place.

In re-cognition, all is actually positioned in terms of relative meaning and significance. Commonly, positioning is established in the "where" of memory as a "fixed place," and in the "when" of memory as "fixed time." Thus a tangible interpretation of The Infinite is possible, but as a sense of fixation or limitation.[19] Also, because significance and meaning is commonly interpreted in terms of space and time, the tangible universe seems to be separate from us. Understandably, the "time" and "place" established in our structuring seems to be outside of us. Hopefully, we will eventually progress to the point where we are free of the idea of fixation. As this occurs, our movements will undoubtedly become less and less restricted.

---

[19] *Perhaps the great distance between us and the stars of outer space indicate how far removed we are from those degrees of realization rather than indicating the common measurement of "light years away" as modern science implies.*

Another factor we must be aware of is the vastness of the structure we call memory. Most of us feel that our memory is our "own" personal record and that each of us holds the only key to that which it contains. This is not true. Each of our memories is shared by all. Perhaps it is our belief systems that create the delusion that our personal awareness is private. We believe we are separate individuals, when actually we are inseparable. There is only one "I." There is only one memory. The universal memory may be likened to a beehive wherein the bees store all the honey they have gathered. It belongs to all the bees. This perhaps accentuates the great importance of the "experience-life" of each and every being and solves the question of our purpose "here." We are gaining the <u>tangible</u> realization of that which we truly are.

To recapitulate just a bit, we can now see that there are two "expanses" or perhaps "domains(?)" in which resides every significance and meaning of The Infinite. One is the all-knowing domain of abstract Cognition which we shall call "Spirit." The second domain is the expanse of re-cognition (Mind), in which all is again, sequentially "laid out" but in tangible terms of significance and meaning. This, in a sense places all the tangible universe into the mental domain we call "memory," and thus allows the recall and reflection that is so essential to the evolvement of tangible Self-realization.

The idea that "that which appears as the physical world and universe may actually be 're-cognition memory'," is probably new to many of us. Yet, we probably do agree that space and time are questionable issues. As we progress, we may come to see them in this different light: "Whenever you recognize something, you must necessarily conceive it in terms of when and where, and how it is significant to you." Otherwise it is meaningless. You then establish it in accordance with your inventory of perceived data. It is positioned in terms of past, present or future, and also located according to significance (what, when, where, how and why) in your mind. Though other factors may be involved, we basically position significance and meaning in terms of space and time. Thus, space and time are conceived.[20]

There is no doubt that, if what is presented here is correct, we are in a situation of perplexity. Similar to the ocean and its drops, we have a strong sense of independence since The Whole itself, is independent, and we fully share all of its qualities. We especially savor our senses of choice and independence. It is easy to see then, how our idea of *separate* identities gives us a problem. We feel we are developing our own, *separate* "I." As has been presented, there is but one Life - one All - one Self - one "I." If that one, infinite "I" were somehow annihilated, we would all disappear.

In this chapter we have primarily illustrated the part that re-cognition played in the tangible creation of the universe, including our creation and the importance of our tangible presence. As most of us realize, there is more to understand about re-cognition, such as the fundamentals of perception and its use. Thinking and its causative nature and the essence of Thought have yet to be fully addressed. The possibility of experiencing realities other than the one we now seem to be locked into bears exploration. We have talked about our birth but not about the idea of death and what actually transpires. The so called sub-conscious mind has not been mentioned, as well as many other pertinent issues such as the male-female syndrome of life,

---

[20] *If it was not for our space and time positioning, there could be only "me," now. There would be no "other." (There would be no other person or thing "out there" to relate to, for ALL would be "here" and "now." All would be intangibly abstract.)*

and the necessity for sleep. The differences of the various races, and color itself, demand exploration. The polarity relationships of positive, negative and neutral and their significance cannot be ignored. Among other things, the structure of cause and effect bears looking into. However, we feel that this book, and what it presents towards the understanding of our true identity, will provide a formidable stepping stone into a more accurate exploration of the seeming mysteries we are surrounded with. The inquisitive mind of the honest student will demand its own investigation.

This Chapter has especially given us much to think about and the mind of the sincere student will surely demand its review until it is thoroughly understood. A later date may find us presenting the results of our research covering those important issues which still demand attention.

SECTOR IX

CONCLUSION

CHAPTER IX

CONCLUSION

There are many who profess allegiance to a metaphysical flag. Various schools such as Astrology, Numerology, Channeling, Tarot reading, etc. as well as a number of cults and some religious organizations have all staked a claim to a degree of metaphysical understanding. There are probably many organizations that have some of the answers. Some intimate that they have all the answers. One wonders if they are aware of all the questions.

Hopefully, with the criteria we have presented, the student has gained a respectful degree of independence from becoming overwhelmed with the presentations of bigoted believers.[21] It is well to realize that each school has its own "inventory of knowledge." To some, an inventory of belief structures, is sufficient and conclusive.

The reasoning and logic presented in this book have dispelled much dependency upon beliefs, but just as with mathematics, its understanding cannot be gained by a casual reading. It will require love and a high degree of honesty to truly study and evaluate what has been presented. If there are flaws in the reasoning, or even if it is altogether wrong (which is a possibility), each student is responsible for their own decision of acceptance or negation.

Let us give thanks to our predecessors who have, in the spirit of love, expended the effort to present what they did in the behalf of

---

[21] *A bigot is not really a dirty word. It portrays someone who has become so enamored of a certain presentation, that they are oblivious to all else.*

those who followed them. Without their efforts, our efforts would probably have missed the target.

Please accept our thanks to you also, for your love and your dedication to honesty. May we all work together to bring forth a continuously higher and higher understanding of the Life that we are.

A TASTE OF FREEDOM

(Author's Note)

If we are willing to accept the responsibility for the thinking we do and the thoughts we hold, we may be interested in a method that teaches us "how to think" rather than "what to think."

Learning the art of "how to think" is simpler than it may seem. The first step is to isolate the *core concepts* that our thinking stems from. A core concept is a basic idea that has been accepted as true. Core concepts are the foundations upon which all of our thinking is built. (The idea "1+1=2" is a mathematical core concept.)

If we can isolate just three of our core concepts it would be a great beginning! What are three basic ideas that we have accepted, that we don't even question anymore? What basic ideas do we now take for granted that we accepted when we were but a child? Is there any basic ideas that we have "socially absorbed?"

Every structure of our thinking can be traced down to a core concept. Once we isolate and then examine our core concepts, we may wish to replace them with new ones, gained from a more mature point of view. *If we felt that we were saddled with them forever, we would demand a closer examination of them!* (We might even wish to allow them room for new growth rather than to shut the door on them as "final.")

It is actually a matter of "think for yourself," or, "let someone else do your thinking for you." It feels good to know you are calling your own shots - "thinking-in" your own mental inventory.

APPENDIX

SECTOR OF POEMS

TABLE OF CONTENTS

POETRY SECTOR

MESSAGES

The cattle in the meadow graze
and move about in the morning haze -
and water flows in clear, cold streams
as buttercups reach for the gleam

of the morning sun. It's nature's grace.
The earth is warmed and we find a place
where we, perhaps, can sit and look -
unobserved, in a grassy nook.

And the swish-swish of a horse's tail
reminds us that the insects sail
about in the sea of air
that's gently tugging at our hair.

And all the action cannot hide
the background quietness that abides -
it's nudging us to wake and find
the hidden beauty in our mind.

AWAKE

"Awake!" oh ye, before your eyes close,
to see what real love holds in store -
for a self-centered outlook gets vision drunk,
and selfishness closes the door...

Oh ye, who scan only surface -
like a hawk, see the <u>face</u> of the earth -
and ye clutch out at earthly possessions,
as if they're of eternal worth...

And ye, who seek but to be entertained -
(and in every possible way),
ye seek for your self, every comfort and joy -
and become satisfied, just to play...

Hear ye, who won't lift a finger -
to dig in the soil of Life -
in our slumbering love, lay the answers,
that applied, could erase worldly strife...

And ye who just stay too busy
to analyze love and its heart -
and to solve "what's more worthy of my precious time,"
can we not make a new start...?

Awake, oh ye, for if ye seek to gain
an honest look at your face -
ALL must be seen, as the "I" of "I AM,"
one "I," held in loving embrace...

and not to be shamed by attention to games
while masses, wilted - starving, view graves -
as we cheer for "our team" and immaturity screams
for the "win," vain humanity craves - -

Awake, oh ye, and see Self, as "We,"
one Self - one "I" - infinite -
we can rise above games that selfishness frames,
and our focus can change, bit by bit...

And ye - oh ye, the children that be -
you've been led to adore glamour's face -
if you don't break the chains of vanity's claims,
what masks will ye seek to embrace...?

Let work be your guide, and achievement your pride -
set a course that will benefit all -
and treat each, just the same, as if they wore your name
oh ye, who would rise to Love's call...

EMPTY YOUR BUCKET?

(Empty your bucket? What does that mean?
"I always thought my bucket was clean!"
Don't I think I'm right, and then "just won't budge,"
especially, when I'm holding a grudge?)

Empty your bucket - and know for your sake,
each interpretation's the one that you make;
and it's easy to say, "The other's to blame,"
for that which you feel, has caused you some shame.

Empty your bucket - though the blame may be "theirs."
Pull yourself up, and then if you dare,
take a good look at "that what's been done."
Do you think you've been harmless to everyone?

Empty your bucket - be first to forgive.
What can you lose - a sad way to live?
Grudges spawn anger which then turns to hate
that lives in your bucket, it's never too late - (to)

Empty your bucket - you're not being insulted -
except in your thoughts, are you being assaulted;
for what's past is past and what's done is done,
and now it rests, as interpretation.

Empty your bucket - What does that mean?
It's <u>'the burden of hatred'</u> that hurts, and demeans.
It is not "they," who are hurting us now -
it's that which still lives in our buckets, somehow - -

Empty your bucket - What do you fear?
What can you lose - a life full of tears?
Have faults become more important than 'good?'
They'd have <u>no</u> life, if only you would -

Empty your bucket - it just weighs you down.
You won't lighten up by nursing a frown.
(Do you really think that grudges can change
what's held in the grip of yesterday's claim?)

Empty your bucket - we're all children as yet.
Let's learn to focus on love, not regret.
Let's not yet expect, of sister or brother,
full perfection in loving each other.

Empty your bucket - why can't you see
the others, touched by your misery?
Those who care, await, undermined
by foolish pride that's keeping you blind.

Empty your bucket - there's a reason why you
were born how you were, and do what you do;
and the same force that governs your fate
is telling you now, you can shed all your hate.

Empty your bucket - Why be so grim
about your condition - the faults and the sins?
Perfection is not expected of you
so why not do as the wiser folks do?

Empty your bucket - when each day is done
and rise up each morning just like the sun,
to refresh and restore, in loving embrace
all that you touch and affect, with new grace - -

Empty your bucket - put blame to bed.
When looking backwards, we can't see ahead!
Can you think of a door to a heavenly life,
that would open to vanity, hatred and strife?

(As we mature, we'll surely become,
acquainted with a new "rule of thumb:"
Hold no thought unless that thought is to be,
worthy of keeping, eternally.)

THE INFINITE "I"

It is "I" that claims us all;
all one "I," one "I" in all.
Why is it so hard to see
the "I," our sole identity?

What could live and what could "die,"
if its essence was not "I,"
in fact, what is it we could be
if "I" did not claim you and me?

And what controls before the womb,
during life and beyond the tomb?
In whose domain, does all Truth lie,
if not the living presence, "I?"

And, if so, must matter be
of the "I" comprising you and me?
Does all "being" then rely
on one, all-inclusive "I?"

The day will come when you will find
the question weighing on your mind -
tugging, forcing you to try
to solve the Truth, regarding "I."

SURRENDER TO UNIFORMITY

Until the Self knows how to walk
it remains prey, for those who stalk
for your control, so many surrender,
to the role, "authority" renders.

If you had children who looked to you
for mental guidance, what would you do
if someone crossed your country's border,
to make them clones for some "new order?"

That, of course, would be easy to do,
for children's minds are not so shrewd
and can be swayed by "ways of kindness,"
leading them to mental blindness.

Religions know that game too well
and in "kindness" cast their spell
to spin us in a web so deep,
that from it, we dare not creep.

From childhood on, they make their play,
implying there's no other way.
They play their hand with "authority" -
we bow our heads, and on bended knees,

look to them for our salvation.
Some of them have conquered nations -
but first they must invade the heart
for that is where they make their start.

"For 'goodness' must you go through them?"
Not so. We need no middlemen
to contact Good, innate in all
awaiting recognition's call - -

Religions prey on the very young -
parents feel good, for what they've done;
they submit to "authority" -
the child is "blessed" while they bend their knee.

And so little, do they know -
for they go, as the masses go,
smugly thinking they're so right
and "belief's" become their sight.

It's amazing how some fight
and even kill, for "what is right;"
and even worse, they close the mind,
of their child, while reason's blind.

The Catholics think, that they stand tall
and Moslems stand within their "walls,"
and Mormons, organized so strong,
may feel that all the rest are wrong.

And most Jews cherish their own clique -
they hang together in their niche.
(We all feel blessed with a special hold
in the Religion we extol.)

Far-Eastern cultures, offer too,
more religions for me and you.
How confusing it must be
to "know the Truth with certainty."

Before you're even born you'll find,
preachers plot to "grab your mind."
They bless everyone they can,
and act like holy middlemen - -

Don't you recognize those "schools"
that turn us into hard-nosed fools -
a "superiority"
of pompous uniformity?

What cowards we must truly be
if we're afraid to look - to see -
if those who brought us up were wrong -
(afraid to find we don't belong).

There are those who went "astray"
and in freedom found the way
to unlock the Truth of Mind
that the others left behind.

Than to "see," like others "see,"
they'd rather live in liberty,
and work to get a view that's clear
of religion's stifling fear.

It may be that there was a day
that religion was "the way" -
when Jesus Christ walked on the earth
and talked about love and its worth.

Why not look at what He said,
through <u>our</u> eyes, and not bow our head
to middlemen who try to sway
the Truth He spoke of, to their way? - -

Will proud preachers ever know
that in honesty, they'll grow
to find that they've been victim, too,
to vanity, like me and you?

For our homework's still not done
'till we discover we're all One;
One Soul, One Truth, our every bit,
for we're all One - - The Infinite.

"It is human to want others to do it 'your' way.
It is Godly to let each do it 'their' way."

Author unknown

DOMINATION

The sun rises early, far out in the East
and shines just the same, on both man and beast,
apparently doing its job just for free
and exactly the same, for you and for me.

It's not making plans for me and for you
and making decisions on what each should do.
It leaves to us, to do what each will.
With free love it shines, and no special deals.

It's in a strong place of authority,
so why don't it choose, just where we should be?
Shouldn't it decide what should be our direction
and manipulate us with its loving affection?

Perhaps in its light, it remains wisely humble
knowing that yoked, the individual must crumble,
and realizes that the individual, to grow,
must make "self-decisions," on terms that it knows;

and though right or wrong the decisions may be,
processed responsibility
thoroughly works to make each one wise,
a maturing, through which, each one will cognize

a lesson, to welcome with no need of fear,
whether bound by false ego, or teachings, austere.
If we manipulate others, in mistaken conceit,
its the individual, who we must cheat - -

to satisfy some sort of unbalanced need -
or perhaps to "be big" in the eyes of a creed
that has yet to mature to the nature of "One."
Can we take a lesson from our friend, the sun?

Just look at our self and the light that we shine.
Did we search it for Truth, or is it memorized line
that we "know" is true because others have said,
that a wiser and higher authority, led

them to believe, what they say, is true,
("so now we can stand much taller than you,
and rob you of what the loving sun won't:
your freedom to choose your own do's and don'ts.")

WHOLLY ONE

Mother and father act as the beast
whose throbbing message of the groin,
brings satisfaction at the least -
and maybe entry, through their loins.

Does animal kingdom reign supreme,
to bring forth the nights and days,
or is God the ruling King
who controls, and calls the plays?

Who decided you'd be born,
and as animal-man attain
a presence in the earthy reign
and at the mercy of a brain -

a brain born with pattern etched
in DNA, to "pave the way" -
a beast that's born to belly hunger,
born to sexually, "make its play?"

To realize God, we go through beast
and the Self within's, the key?
We suffer through the earthly life
to find our true identity?

Our vision focusses on love,
for what we love, is what we deem
important to retain in sight -
important to our self-esteem.

We see with the eyes of an animal
a world of jumbled wants and fears -
some that tend to make us fall,
yet we develop, through the years - -

Could there be more than meets the eye
and the Truth yet hides, in Time?
Could "the animal" be a lie,
and an experience, sublime -

to unfold all, that we can be
and are waiting to become -
to prepare us all to see,
that we all, are wholly, One?

Our life, through "manly-animal,"
confusing as it all may seem -
will know God as "One - The All"
though for now, it seems a dream.

TEMPLE SANCTUARY

The lake of Life seems frozen now
and we know that we must cross, somehow -
some have tried but the ice broke through
and where they're at, we have no clue.

We walk on the ice, and the ice gets thin,
and we think 'bout Life, and death, and sin,
and we feel restless, me and you
for we wonder, if we'll fall in too.

If so they'll look for us, in vain
and most won't even know our name -
forgotten soon and not much said
when we're remembered as "the dead."

"Where did they go, what shall we do?"
is the question asked of you,
if you haven't died as yet.
And no-one really can forget

that death's a mystery indeed
and towards which, all footsteps lead,
for they all point to the vertical cave -
the home of corpses, called "the grave."

How can we see beyond the veil?
What hides from us - why do we fail
to somehow grasp the reality -
the actual reason for a "me?"

We cower and huddle with our heads bent,
and pray for answers - Heaven sent.
In the church of religious authority
we praise or beg, on bended knee - -

As if we can't solve the Truth on our own,
we settle for words, by religious clones.
"To reach God" we use preachers - as middlemen,
since most of them imply that "they can."

Each Sunday we gather in groups and sit,
and feel a fear that we won't admit -
we wonder about immortality
and "If after my death, will I cease to be?"

The fear abides deep in our core
and like sheep, when they sense a predator
we huddle together restlessly
and praise God for our sense of security.

Then we clothe ourselves with feelings, smug -
but the graveyards have the hole all dug
to receive the body we surrender,
(perhaps the corpse of a family member).

And at the church we congregate
and they tell us, of our destined fate,
if we don't behave in the prescribed way
and memorize what they have to say.

Majestic temples rise up, tall
but like the rest, someday they'll fall,
for time has proven to all men
that its happened time and time again.

We seem to flounder helplessly
because we've learned dependency -
on another, to choose our way
tradition tells us what to say - -

So be politically correct -
and if you hope to resurrect,
"lose your individuality
but enhance your name-identity."

"And when you do, you can go through me -
the Temple that trapped your loyalty
and cost you your thinking ability -
with a counterfeit sense of security."

Drink only their milk, in the nest of their rules -
don't think for yourself - remain as fools.
"Be somebody" by pleasing the clones,
stay loyal to temples of bricks and stones.

In the dark, the corpses lay
but darker yet is our dismay
since Truth's unsolved, 'bout "God and Me" -
we've slighted opportunity.

Why look for camaraderie
with a religious, *believing* humanity,
who don't realize that Truth is free -
that it resides in each heart, and thee and me?

THE ROAD OF DESTINY

Our restless feet will walk the streets
hoping they will somehow meet
fulfillment of what needs to be
on the road of destiny.

Old age is knocking at our door
and we wonder what's in store
when our feet stop dancing to the tune
that will be ending very soon.

And our minutes are numbered now
a fact that's been ignored somehow.
With stony face we do our best -
as love's put to another test.

Destiny will make its call
as the worldly curtain falls -
Revealing what? Where will we be?
Is there any kind of security?

And a bottle of wine, takes the pressure off
as we clear our throat with a drunken cough -
the words we say are what others said,
for we're somehow stuck in the human bed.

So we amuse ourselves and seek out fun
and forget our worldly end to come -
Why look for Truth that may set us free?
Its easier to watch T-V.

ESCAPE

What is death, but the great escape
from ignorance we've had to face.
No longer must we struggle now
to feed and clothe ourselves somehow.

Old age, decay, disease and death
are blamed for claiming our last breath
but each of us in our hearts, know;
we failed to learn - we failed to grow -

into the knowledge that brings peace
by understanding West and East,
and North and South, and all we find -
in terms of Truth - in terms of 'Mind.'

Oh to understand, just what God is,
instead of quoting "that" or "this"
and putting on religious airs!
How many search? Yet most must care,

for they submit to religious fools
who use their bibles as their tools
to lull the masses into sleep -
their fancy temples housing sheep.

We fought each other, for "our way,"
while vanity reigned and had free play -
our search for Truth was set aside
and we looked around for an easy ride.

Is it better or is it worse?
Is it a blessing or a curse?
<u>Is</u> it the way that religions say,
or have we, like fools, been led astray? - -

There are answers we've not found,
yet where, but "here," could Truth abound?
Is our death false, or is it a way
for us to escape, when we've had our say?

The door that opens "just one way"
acts to carry us away
to an abstract life, thats now surmised -
a reality, disguised.

Then, will our new eyes see the light
we failed to see in broad daylight?
Will our minds be open, so new doors
can open up to show us more?

THE ONE SOUL

The present time - "our earthly stay,"
let's us know we're on our way -
to where? Is humus birth
a blended Self, of Soul and Earth?

What does it take - what must I be,
to validate my identity?
How do I identify,
the mystic Self, that I call "I?"

What awareness must I gain,
to claim for Self, an eternal name?
(Is it a part, or is it the Whole -
the consciousness, I call, "my Soul?")

If the self "I know and see,"
is not a full identity
and only a "part" of a unity,
then what is to become of me?

Is my presence here, for real?
Can man, himself, be made to "feel,"
or are we parts of "a unified One,"
and like "a living note," we come

into being on earthly stage,
as a fleshy entourage -
and like notes that enter songs -
we fade away, when we don't belong?

(And then once more, are we ushered in
to be born again, as human kin?)
Can your Soul, then, once more claim,
an earthly brand - a human name? - -

Do we cycle back to the "Infinite Song,"
to await new birth, when "our note" belongs,
(to enrich the "Song" - and not, our name)
and live as the "I" of Eternal claim?

("Notes" have no meaning if by themselves -
the "song" itself, is their "Soul," their "Self.")
Through Infinite presence, the Whole stays whole -
but do its "notes" comprise its Whole?

The only full presence? The Whole - "The One" -
The Whole - whose Will, will ever be done.
Only one "I" - one identity -
living as you and living as me.

Somehow the powers that be,
establish the births of "The Infinite Me"
so it can understand and identify
the one and the only, "Infinite I."

THE ABSTRACT "I"

Just how can reality be,
in the finiteness of me,
unless the finiteness of me
is really not reality?

The limits of perceptiveness
all yield to our forgetfulness
and can't be real because they fade
no matter how well they've been made.

Nothing lasts except the Truth -
just look at our expiring youth
(and even that which lives in memory
seems to fade into obscurity).

So is our perception wrong?
How <u>did</u> our presence come along?
What happened to the "I" of me,
to effect the changes that I see?

And if I'm living in a dream,
are things unlike that which they seem -
and await my freedom from addiction
to an animal perception -

of a beast who walks on an earthly reign
where predators command domain -
where something must die, for something to live
and death somehow serves as the means to give -

and like hawks, we clutch at our bleeding prey
and slowly peck its life away.
Is "all" shared eventually,
to feed the belly of a greater "me?" - -

Is <u>this</u> what I'm really doing here -
feeding a Mind that's still obscure
about the Truth in which it reigns
and the "realities" it claims?

Oh, my son, why can't it be
that somehow we could clearly see,
just what the "I" can really be,
when will we solve this mystery?

Please remember (and you can bet that it's true),
when you bring them your money, casinos "love" you.

SOMETHING FOR "FREE"

"Something for nothing -
something for free -
at another's expense
and at no cost to me."

That is the dream
that the gamblers must choose,
as they wait with the hope
that they'll win, and not lose.

And, like wine blots out reason,
they're consumed with their dream -
you don't dare interfere
as they play their machines.

But a price must be paid -
and confusion will reign,
when machines deal the cards
in a pre-programmed game -

computerized monsters,
that pay out, with a crash -
and the bells keep a-ringing
while you furnish the cash.

The magical word,
is the mystical "FREE!"
It means, "something for nothing,"
and greed is the key - -

But if you do "win,"
someone must lose,
yet the house gets its cut
(and keeps buying the booze).

And - just like honey's
a lure for the bee,
the promise of riches
acts hypnotically.

A nickel, a quarter
a few bucks will do,
"This machine's got to hit!"
("And the odds favor you?")

And, so what if you lose?
You can allay your fear -
(oh, they're so good to you,
these casinos, "so dear") -

they'll help you save money
for a "luckier" day -
(go fill up your belly
at the bargain buffet!)

More casinos are built,
as their riches accrue -
and with the money of <u>losers</u>
they "accommodate" you.

But its not really you
its your greed that they want.
The real you, knows better,
its your greed that they taunt - -

They somehow know,
greed immaturely,
puts a spell over love,
and "just looks out for me."

The wise in their hearts
really know its their shame,
when they seek out their riches
through gambling games.

They know its not right
if another must pay
for their gain without works -
though it might "make their day."

And their conscience will tell them
what they're doing is wrong,
and they'll finally realize
that "it just don't belong."

Then - they'll look for a game
in which everyone gains -
a win, win condition
where all's very plain,

with all cards "face up" -
and where each one can see,
"what's in it for you"
and "what's in it for me."

'til then, they'll mature
until they can see,
its a lie - there's no truth
in the myth known as "free" - -

Yet, how long will we go on
allowing a lie,
to justify that
which in truth, we deny?

Each heart has the answer,
for each yearns to be free
of the selfishness, bound up
in all falsity.

TRAPPED

So I walk into the parlor
and I turn on my T-V
and see pictures of the people
moving 'round like you and me.

They don't know where they come from -
they don't know where they've been -
they've got fur (that they call hair),
and a covering called "the skin."

They hide and scream and jump about,
'bout what? They think they know -
for their life's of great importance,
(they're members of a show).

They resemble animals,
all caught up in a strife
of hurts and wants and pleasures,
for their body is their life.

They're trapped inside their bodies -
a fact that they ignore;
they seem to be too busy
to investigate their "core."

There are those that do profess,
to knowing the way out.
They put on religious airs
and plead, or rant and shout:

"Come into our shelter,
We know! We'll set you free -
believe our special story,
get immortality" - -

They're locked inside their bodies
and the women paint their face;
the men all strut their fancy stuff -
they sidestep the disgrace

that they don't have the freedom
to go past skin and bones -
(an ignored imprisonment,
inside their aging "homes").

But there's no getting comfortable
with what we've got to face -
old age - decay - the sicknesses,
of the flesh we all embrace.

So more and more are looking for,
the way that is above -
dependency on the animal-man,
the life we've learned to love.

"I only hope it comes to be,
that the hand of God focussed as "me,"
prevails unto maturity
as a guiding light for "we."

-- *Athanasios*

THE HAND OF GOD

The child's face glows with a smile
and radiates love - and it stares for a while
with wonder filled eyes, as it plays in the sand -
Could it be, its aware of the touch of God's hand?

Across the street, his money he counts -
the beggar - measures his worth by amounts
of coin he's secured, in a generous land
where all is sustained by the touch of God's hand -

a Grace, that the beggar's not yet defined -
except perhaps, in the progressing mind
of the child within him, an entity grand,
that lives in the realm of God's guiding hand.

That arrogant look, remote and discreet -
displayed on the faces of some folks we meet -
is fear-filled aloofness, defensively bland -
(yet, behind the mask, is the touch of God's hand).

Resentment, anger and fear make their play,
in the selfish outlook some would portray -
yet innate to each, like the crystal in sand
is the ever abiding, touch of God's hand - -

Pride or vanity, or sheer selfishness
claiming residence at our address
can't overshadow the fact that we stand
always, inside the grip of God's hand.

Those hearts filled, not with love, but with hate
will find one day, that the storms of that fate
evolve into love that they'll understand;
for each is endowed, with the touch of God's hand.

Mistaken action - all we've done wrong -
repeats itself 'til it "just don't belong;"
and each who has grown at wisdom's command
knows we've been blessed, by the touch of God's hand.

Infinite Grace can never be lost
to an immature posture that we accost
in our experience - woman or man -
for guiding us each, is the touch of God's hand.

THE HUMAN CLUTCH

Born a baby with no say,
and "victimized" by DNA -
reaching out with hands and lips
to grasp and hold in "beastly grip,"

the breast that fills the present need
and nourishes the growing seed.
(Somehow, most seem satisfied
to let dependency abide.)

"The grip of flesh!" so some would say,
when they try to break away
from the intense craves and needs
that DNA plants in the seed.

And the fittest will survive -
but do they really stay alive,
or as "flashes in the pan,"
wait, 'til "old age" plays its hand?

Some feel that they have no say,
being born a "slave" to DNA -
it seems a reason - or serves as such,
to stay in the grasp of the human clutch.

"Why look for something that's above
dependencies we've learned to love?
Only fools would ever stray,
from comfort zones of human ways."

But "living" flesh soon does decay,
and there is a better way.
True Self, from DNA is free
and dwells in self-sufficiency - -

but if it's stopped at sensual touch,
it's grounded by the human clutch,
and yet awaits, most patiently
for Love and Truth to set it free.

There are those who won't surrender
to the "child" that they remember,
but find new needs to gratify -
their Godly Self to satisfy.

A GRATEFULNESS

Every day, I must express
my perpetual gratefulness
For Love and Truth, and choice that's clear
for joy, and gladness, and good cheer.

And every moment of my life,
even if it holds some strife,
finds a way to let me know
that problems help each one to grow.

It's up to me to run my mind -
to take control of what I find,
and let no other be my voice,
by robbing me of my own choice.

It's a loving quest for me
to try to solve the mystery
of my presence in this world;
to associate with boys and girls -

grown-ups (some so set in mind),
and animals of every kind.
What more is it I could ask,
than to face the pleasing task

of opening the door of mind
to explorations we may find,
could touch us all in Love and Truth,
and enrich the searching mind of youth?

Yes, I am grateful I am here;
right here, right now, and in good cheer,
and grateful for my destiny
of sharing with humanity - -

the issues that can help us show
each other new ways we can grow,
free, from old chains of tradition
and gaining for us the admission

to a reign of self that's far above
the lesser life we've learned to love.
I'm grateful there's a way to see
the issues of infinity.

CONTROL

Creator, law or providence,
intelligence or common sense,
the force that somehow keeps us whole,
adds up to just one thing: control.

Some call it God, or Lord, or Grace,
the Force that somehow, made their face -
but could it be, that <u>all</u> life holds,
is summed up in the word, "control?"

For how could your life make a stand
if it was not kept well in hand?
Or do you think its "hocus pocus"
that keeps consciousness in focus?

And whose focus are we in?
Is it called "The force within?"
Is it our's or another's choice
that brings forth words, for us to voice?

How could you be separate from,
the focus that maintained your mom?
(And <u>if</u> separate, you must surely be
a total self-sufficiency.)

But if "separate" means to isolate,
and separation <u>is</u> your state,
this means you could touch and see,
only that which you call, "me."

What do we know about control
of identity - our soul;
does another hold the key,
or is it ours, essentially? - -

Somehow, control seems to be
the same control for you and me;
and like the bee supports the hive,
we help each other to survive.

We're all breathing the same air -
somehow have the world to share,
though time takes its deadly toll,
and the newborns gain "control."

To find out, what's truly, "me,"
we must search "eternity,"
for the Truth can never change -
eternally, it stays the same.

Has our reasoning been wrong?
Is that why it takes so long -
(life-times spent - experiencing)
what does "control" really mean?

ADDITION TO WYOMING STATE HOSPITAL (CORRECTIVE PSYCHIATRY)

It was in "big, wide, wonderful" Wyoming
'bout the year 1973
where I got down to a dime,
and so, sold my time, to the 'Western States Masonry.'

And what is more noble than labor?
for you know when you're doing your share,
you're using your might, to do what is right;
there's no question, you're doing "what's fair."

The job was cluttered with angles,
and complications that it takes time to see -
a building made fitting to do the mind's bidding,
"Corrective Psychiatry."

And the walls that we slowly are raising,
do they know of what use they will be?
a doctor can look, but does he find in a book
living answers for you and for me?

One day I looked at my trowel,
a useful, historical tool;
then I looked straight at me and tried hard to see,
is it held by a man or a fool?

Has it covered up any problems,
that could have been handled "now,"
or has it left for another, a future of struggle,
of correcting my errors, somehow?

And is not each mind also cluttered
with that which it takes time to see?
and who, at one time or another,
has not questioned their own sanity? - -

Who knows, but what all endeavors aren't actually good,
for much may be masked don't you see,
by the directing hand, which we don't understand,
our true, identity -

(and is identity claimed by a figure, or form,
as seen from reflected light?)
Mental illusion will yield to confusion;
who knows the answer that's right?

You do know that now, you have grown somehow,
and your structure, like the buildings, stands high;
and despite fears and troubles, mistakes and the struggles,
you can say that your life's not a lie.

Someday we will find the answer,
to exactness and refinement of skill,
applied to each man, with that which can,
bring out truth, and let error stand still.

Until then, I'll stick to my trowel,
and I reckon I'll do what I can,
to be of some service (and not get too nervous),
for I'm a 'Western States Masonry' man.

RELIGIOUS COWBOY HAT

Is it true that we are proud, of "knowing where it's at,"'
when all we may have ever done, is wear a cowboy hat
that parents and society have laid upon our head,
and questioned not, its meaning, until perhaps we're "dead?"

And did our parents really know their cowboy hat would fit?
And did they really care, as long as we would sit
just like a good and loyal dog, content to chew on bones
and fit into the pattern of some well-intentioned clones?

For if you wear a cowboy hat, "A cowboy you must be!"
and there's plenty more just like you, to keep you company.
They say that "You are one of us," and you may take great pride
in thinking just as they do, and be taken for a ride.

A horse is chosen for you, by those who "know much more,"
"and who are you to choose," when it's they who "know the score?"
And are they not exalted as knowing more than you,
because they've *memorized* what they and you should do?

To "seek and know the Truth through Self," is not repeated now;
"just listen to the story that we've *memorized* somehow,
and question not what's given you, and listen to 'just that,'
follow and obey the rules, (and wear your cowboy hat)!"

"And now that you're a cowboy, you stay inside your stall,
and don't you peek through the corral, or you will surely fall."
Be like the goodly Moslem, who kneels and bows each day,
in the given manner, when told that "it's the way."

(And if you think you're better, just look at where you sit -
were you branded by consent, or did you "just submit?")
If you want to be accepted, "tradition shows the way,"
and "the sacredness of our script," will tell you what to say. - -

To bring more cowboys to the fold, you must be organized,
into a plan of telling, the "Truth" you've memorized.
So go out and knock on doors, and more will wear your brand,
but before you tell another, have you *really* checked your hand?

And if you don't obey, the rules of your corral,
the implication is, there's some sure kind of hell
awaiting you at death, but it's applied each day,
for ostracism plays its hand in very subtle ways.

The sword is not their weapon - its fear that's put to use
and it's their pecking order, that heaps on more abuse.
Guilt trips 'bout your children are another weapon too,
(but there's nothing more exalted, than the Truth you find for you.)

Deep down in their heart, each wants to do what's right
but are they strong enough to see that love's been spent as fright?
Can they forgive their loved ones, and those who helped them stay,
in the stifling corrals, while searching for the way?

THE PURPOSE OF ANIMAL-MAN

From the Whole, known as "The God Entity,"
comes a world - - full of identities.
Personalities - embodied souls,
assume that a role in support of the Whole

is their fate, and maybe they're right;
for all entities live by the might
of the Whole, and though they don't understand,
they gratefully place their feet on its land.

We call our fur, hair - we don't care to admit
our animal structure; we feel that we're fit
to be a bit more, so we glamorize;
we wear clothes and paint, as a sort of disguise.

(But for something to live, must not something die?)
Is our animal body therefore a lie,
since it don't last through eternity,
and can be eaten into obscurity?

And what happens, to that which is learned
of desire and love - the sexual yearn,
that transmitted seed in another to thrive,
and be newly born in the animal hive?

We laugh and we joke and we strut in our name -
and rejoice, in our cherished animal frame
of which we're so proud, yet know little about
'though there's a Truth, that could still all our doubts,

by presenting the life that stands far above
the animal life that we've learned to love.
Is not our life glutted by doubts and by fear?
How many rely on liquor for cheer - -

or excess of food or measures unkind,
or step on others as they strive to find
the animal type of security -
a need that is based on fear or on greed?

And what's so important 'bout a "you," and a "me?"
Why do we struggle "eternally"
to search out a Truth that "we'll never die?"
(We must suspect that we're more than a lie.)

Who is the "Who" that's holding the reins
of the death that we, as animals, claim?
Will that which survives of a personal "me,"
live only in thought, as a past memory?

In our whole life, what is it that counts,
if none care enough to explore the fount,
of that which is called, 'our true origin?'
What is the reason why we have been

born, into this world full of wonder,
with its mornings and nights - its lightning and thunder?
Could our mission be to search and to scan?
(We're born, as *self-conscious*, animal-man.)

Is it only "we" that *can* form a word?
Is it only "we" that *can* talk, and are heard?
Is it only "we" that *can* claim a name?
Why should we "die" then, of old age, in shame?

If thinking's our function, how long has it been
since we've examined our origin?
Or, do we escape from our thoughts of survival
by focussing on our new-born arrivals - -

who, bearing our names as "the pride of the clan"
are branded at birth, as an "animal-man"?
(And now we can feel we've an "ace in the hole,"
for "Our name will last!" - we're not sure of soul.)

Our soul, we deal with, in terms of conjecture,
perhaps based on hope and religious lecture.
We want to live, forever, we hope,
with the wisdom of genius, and "plenty of rope."

How much time do we spend, each day and night,
stroking our bodies, our minds, and our sight
with the hopes and the claims of the animal clan?
(Will we *ever* make it past animal-man?)

The only way that we'll ever know,
if Truth lies in the path that we've chosen to go,
is to question each "fact" for its "what" and its "why,"
and reach for the full *understanding* of "I."

Do you think death ever brings one to see
what the Truth is, 'bout the Self you call "me?"
If so, then death is smarter than life,
so why not just die, and end all the strife?

Perhaps we will find that there is no death,
and living does not depend on our breath,
but to a power we don't understand
and somehow attribute to animal-man.

The Infinite "I," aspires to be
re-cognized, eternally
and yet it knows, this cannot be done
in terms of a single, homogenous One - -

Relativity then, is a state
of tangibility, that is innate
in the Whole, that does demand "parts,"
and maybe that's, where we had our start.

Are we not the eyes and ears of the Whole
to *re*-cognize Truth and Love as its soul
and so, establish God-infiniteness
as tangible structures of consciousness?

Though into existence as babies we come,
we innately know, that our source is one;
and in this 'knowing,' we'll find that we can
better serve God, as an animal-man

that will, one day, progress to a state
of matured-Self, in line with its fate
to understand how God is the "I,"
and not "matter-bodies" that wither and die.

Though in relative state, we truly can say,
we actually are of "God-DNA."
Each will progress, in the best way they can,
to the true understanding of animal-man.

FLESH AND BONES

Skeletons that walk on earth,
with flesh that clings like clothes, at birth -
fleshy pleasure - fleshy pain
memories housed in a fleshy brain.

Fleshy clothes on human bones
that identify the clones -
see the fleshy evidence
of identity and scent.

And the grip of flesh on bones
provides a signature in tones -
a temporal identity,
established as a "he" or "she" -

and the image we embrace,
presents to us, a changing face.
What is our true identity?
Who is the "I," I call a me?

(And what is it that moves the bones?
What satisfaction cries and moans
for a carnal fulfillment -
flesh for an attirement?)

INFINITE MATURITY

In order to understand its Soul -
its oneness, and its sole control -
The Whole Self - The Infinite -
experiences Self - as its every bit.

How long will God extend its stay,
and play its hand in the human way -
so it can stock its memory,
with all life's possibilities,

and experience to the fullest measure,
every pain and every pleasure
of human life and its taste of death,
with its anxious gasp for a final breath?

Its an endless stream of composites,
derived through the play of "opposites" -
each face and action, serving as clue,
towards the understanding, of what's true.

And the mystic touch of flesh
with its mysterious caress,
must too, serve some essential role
in the purpose of The Whole.

And time and space - relativity?
Each a factor of eternity -
God's necessities, demanding
distinctions, for its understanding.

(The distinctions of tangibility,
light up the face of Infinity -
and bring forth the *reason*, for every grace
in The Infinite embrace.) - -

And only intelligence can guide,
for only intelligence abides -
and Love, the pulse of The Infinite
is the heartbeat of life in each part and bit.

Time and space then will survive
as framework, through which love derives
each step - progressing fearlessly -
towards Infinite maturity.

SOMEHOW

Somehow the focus I call "soul"
requires a body, so it "shows."
But if my body was to "die,"
what then, would I call an "I?"

Somehow, it must be a lie
when someone says that "I" will die,
for that would mean obliteration
of the world I call sensation,

and somehow, render meaningless
the efforts where I did my best
as child, adult and as a youth,
to love and understand the Truth.

Somehow, the mind in which "I," hides,
seems fully open on all sides,
so why is it, so hard to see
the force that's in control of me?

Somehow, I feel that knowledge waits
to light the darkness of a fate
where recognition based on error,
ushers in a world of terror.

Somehow, recorded memory
may be all, I take with me
through the change that we call "death,"
when bodies draw their final breath.

Somehow, I feel animal-man,
of itself, will never scan
Intelligence that gives it birth,
unless it knows of Godly worth.

"And so, my son,

Let us reflect. Is it not a feeling of self-insecurity that forces us to grovel for attention and acceptance?"

--Athanasios

SELF AGGRANDIZEMENT ("big-shot-itis")

Born as a baby, a destiny -
of introduction to a "me,"
that clamors to make its presence known -
it somehow knows its not alone.

"Notice me!" it pleads in tears
and its mother calms its fears
as she bares her milky breast
and the child does the rest,

to lay claim to its warm meal -
a gift of motherhood - it feels
the warmth of her embrace,
and the softness of her face.

The words of praise and love it hears,
are a memory held dear
as it struggles for its space
of acclaim in the human race.

"Notice me! Oh, look!" it pleads,
as it performs its special deeds.
It learns to talk, then "walk a fence"
and to hold its mother in suspense - -

Its glad to know "somebody cares"
but it finds it's hard to share
the attention to a "me,"
so hard-won, it's misery

when another baby's born
and the singular love is torn,
to be shared with another's face;
and so, it learns of a shared embrace -

and its view begins to change;
it focusses on a new range -
"if others can think well of me,
then that, will be my specialty."

It then starts looking far and wide,
for applause - a wounded pride
seeks restoration and solace -
an audience - a close embrace.

To be accepted is one thing,
but to be a "star's," more promising.
Sports are fine, and music too,
"to 'prove' no-one's better than you."

To be a "groupie" is one way -
just "hang out" with those, each day,
who've gained applause in world esteem,
and their "glory" will redeem

your pride, and though, phony it be,
you'll feel like an "important me;"
and any group can be "your band."
(Religious groups keep well in hand - -

"groupies," who pay well for grace
bestowed upon their smiling face,
and "self-importance" is restored -
not by works - but through "group accord.")

If joining groups becomes our way
to gain "prestige," with those whose sway,
of seeming "status" means so much -
the Self we are, gets out of touch.

The young or foolish, sometimes seek
to join a gang on a city street,
or even drug-gangs in some school,
and let their minds be led by fools

whose desperation "to belong,"
has set them on a road that's wrong -
that will surely "clip their wings" -
and stunt them from developing

the love that's deep inside their hearts
and don't know where to make its start -
but would, if they would wait with grace,
and give it time to show its face.

Yes, every action has its price,
and redemption's not so nice,
when to Self, we know we've lied,
and honest motive is denied.

A "seek Truth" goal could set us free
from a life of vanity,
for our life is surely meant
to be more than self-aggrandizement - -

In our hearts each knows what's right
and sometimes, it takes all our might
to ignore our "friends," and "talk,"
and "pointed fingers," as we walk,

into the life that <u>we</u> can claim
with our achievements, not praise-fame
from immature mouths, that secretly,
may be looking out "for only me."

(Born a baby, we do fall,
but rise again and though we stall,
the time will come when we'll be free,
of the "need" for praise and flattery.)

OUR RULING LOVE

What is it that constitutes
our cue, to act as God or brute?
Are thoughts not drawn from "up above,"
in submission to our ruling love?

Thought may precede our every action,
but it looks to feeling for direction,
for without love, thought cannot be,
unified meaningfully.

If sad, our thoughts are negative,
and if glad, our thoughts are positive,
and few realize, just how suave,
is the action of our ruling love.

Subtly, love plays its hand
and reason fights to make a stand,
to find what's true and make correction
of wrong thought, held by affection.

For love of anger and revenge
brings forth the thought "Avenge! Avenge!"
and if love but plants *that* seed,
we plot to satisfy *that* need;

and if satisfied, we call *that* "good."
because, "they got just what they should!"
Enjoyment readjusts its sights,
and love keeps saying that "It's right!"

Yes - our ideas of "what is good,"
rest upon the things that would
fulfill the need our love decides,
but if that love is based on lies...? - -

Is it immaturity
that allows a "joy" of enmity
to blind us to the unbound wealth
of the Godly virtues of the Self?

Perhaps it's time for us to find
the key to what controls our mind
through "whispered" cues, or perhaps a shove?
It's time we looked at our ruling love.

BEAUTIFUL INDIVIDUALITY

When I look in the mirror, what do I see?
Do I see the truth of the image called "me,"
or do I long for glamour and then bow my head
to fuss at my hair until I go to bed?

When I turn from the mirror, am I satisfied
with the designs and styles that others decide?
Is it other's opinions that "make me first rate,"
telling me what to like, and what I "should" hate?

If it's beauty (or less), that does "make my case,"
who's capable then, of judging my face?
Who really knows what should be admired?
Is glamour for real, or belief that's acquired?

They may call you "ugly," or "pretty" or "cute,"
"mediocre or "so-so," or "that handsome brute,"
but the only opinion that's worthy of you
is the one that you, in your heart, know is true.

It's the one that's not sold through Hollywood fame,
or beauty contests with counterfeit claims,
that misguide most (and maybe us too?)
into thinking that beauty's unique to a few.

The wise do see real beauty in each
and know, that the grasp of that special reach
into existence (that's known as a "me"),
truly needs copy no other to be

of the highest order of esteem and worth -
They know that all is endowed, through our birth -
a portrayal to all that's special to see,
our own individuality.

THE REALITY OF "I"

Whether boldly or in disguise,
each day, the question will arise:
"What's my real identity -
who, or what, is really me?"

It prevails like the scent of food -
always there, like a hidden mood -
for, like the truth behind each lie,
there's a reality to "I."

The "I" of me and the "I" of you -
are they but one, or are they two?
Are apples, hanging on a tree,
all parts of the tree, or a sovereignty?

If the "I" is our family tree,
are we "I-apples," all named "me?"
Is God the "tree-I," and holding all -
and the <u>only</u> "I" - and alive as all?

Oh, how do I identify,
the Self, that seems to live and die?
Is there a new way we can try -
to get an honest look at "I?"

THE MARK OF THE BEAST

The eyes of the beast become panicky
when searching out "what's in it for me,"
"Me - all for me, until I'm deceased!"
denotes the selfish mark of the beast.

The swine grunt and squeal in delight at the trough,
but somehow their bellies don't get enough,
to satisfy cravings based on their greed
for they cannot settle for just what they need -

but grovel for more, at another's expense
as they belly their way into offensive stance -
and none stop to knock at courtesy's door,
as they trample on others - swine to the core.

The lion searches the jungle to feast
on the life of another - the mark of the beast -
its eyes focus hard on the meal that is living;
the beast thrives on taking rather than giving.

In the city, the dollar sign reigns
obsessing minds and bodies and brains,
with financial hunger and those with the least,
are not immune to the mark of the beast.

How many grunt and squeal at the trough
where public money's never enough
to satisfy cravings based on their greed?
And work is ignored, so long as they feed

on the love and the sweat and the labor of those,
who in the aura of dignity chose
to carry the weight of work on their back,
though they, too well, know the meaning of lack - -

And the financier searches to feast
off the sweat of another - the mark of the beast,
and credit's extended and those who do work
pay dues to the one whose money lurks

in the shadows, seeking its prey -
interest - blood money, that paves the way,
for the beast to walk in the working man's door,
clutching a pen, and lusting for more.

Yes, the eyes of the beast, become panicky
when searching out "what's in it for me,"
"Me - all for me, until I'm deceased!"
denotes the selfish, mark of the beast.

The eyes of the wise, look for what's done
towards the good and advancement of everyone,
and know that true love would surely cease
were we to live by the mark of the beast.

For what is grander than we do not fail
to learn of the message all sages hail?
"Unto others, do and become
as if you, yourself, were everyone."

NAME-IDENTITY

And so, my son, the child grows
into its destiny - who knows
just where its steps will lead?
And each mother shields her seed

and gives it of her very best
as it develops in its nest
of human frailty,
crying to fill its every need.

Character's important, yes,
but survival's its first test,
and, animalistically,
it yields to selfishness and greed.

Identified by human name
self-advancement is its game.
It focusses on "me and mine"
and the religion it defines

as "the one that's tried and true,"
and therefore right for me and you -
with its promise of eternity
for our name-identity.

We cherish our name-identity!
"A great intellect - a glamorous me"
struts its stuff, yet stands in line,
to be ravaged by old age and time - -

When we do get past our name -
past the animal-man we frame
past the mask, we call a me,
then we may know our real self, free -

Free to grow in forgivingness,
and to bask in gratefulness,
to the Self thats more than mesh
of face and bones and fragile flesh.

"Work for the hive and let the hive work for you;
accept the love of The Whole, and not just the few."

MY FAMILY

Look at them! They're just flesh and bones,
with perhaps freckled skins or deep colored tones,
light or dark hair, and eyes dark to grey;
and just who they are, can we really say?

Could they be the cast from some sort of dream,
or are they more than that which they seem?
Could it be, they are some part of me?
Is it right that I call them, "My family?"

They're skin and bones, and they're flesh and blood,
and their structural elements are about like the mud.
To converse with them I find easy to do,
but who is the "who" that I'm talking to?

Just where does the "I" of each one begin?
Do you think "I"- can be bound, by a skin?
Have you thought 'bout one "I" being all there might be,
and living through all, discriminately?

Does the hive own the bees, or do the bees own the hive?
Without the one, could the other survive?
Is this how one "I" is of essence to me
and that without its life, mine never could be?

In thinking ourselves separate identities,
we limit the "I" to the claim of a "me,"
or a false family claim of just "me and mine,"
(and in limited ways, we think we've done fine.) - -

Yes, we can learn from the life of the bee,
the lesson of just one validity,
and sense one, Whole Self while adjusting our sight;
for "I am the Way, and the Truth and the Life."

Take no thought unless that thought is to be,
worthy of keeping, eternally;
and in looking for truths of how you've "begun,"
you may find that "I," and "The Father," are one.

DEATH

To escape from the human wound
<u>must</u> we be fitted for a tomb?
In order to live, must something die,
or is our death, somehow a lie?

Must I gasp for my last breath -
and feel the claws of the grip of death
before I drop my vanity
to seek my real identity?

The acrid smell of human sweat
denotes the struggle "to get - to get!"
Personal power prods and sways
the public crowd - the masses lay

in the grip of sleep, Self-abandonment -
too busy to seek what their life meant -
too busy walking in "personal shoes"
to look for the meaning in a "who."

How to escape from a miserable breath
and how to enter the sleep of death
and how to grasp life, by what's not known
and how to live when you're all alone -

Is that what death demands of you?
Must you be all alone to do
what's required, to really know -
where you've been and where you'll go?

And so, what dies? Is it personal power?
A measurement - of minutes and hours?
Just what will you take with you
when you finally bid this world, "adieu?" - -

Who is it that marks the day
when your shadow finds its way
beyond the darkness where its been,
to the sunshine of its origin -

in search of true identity
in search of true reality
in search of that, that's not a dream
in search of light that won't demean?

Does not the welcome of escape
demand that we all be awake
to Truth today - so we can share -
with whoever else is waiting "there?"

THE ONE AND ONLY "I"

"I" am the part, and "I" am the Whole,
and tangibility is my role.
I'm the same "I" in both mother and daughter
and I'm that same "I" in each drop of water.

It may be classed as an ignorant lie,
when somebody says that "You" is not "I,"
and when you look at distinctions, apart,
just know that "I," am the life of each part.

The "I" of the whole, as hive is to bee,
lives as <u>each</u> part, if "I" is "to be."
The Whole can only see Self, through its "I's,"
for the "part" is really the Whole, in "disguise."

The "I" to be whole, <u>must</u> live through all,
or its "parts," into a remoteness would fall -
a scattered puzzle, of course, is not whole,
can you not see, that the Whole, is your Soul?

It's "I-gravity" that holds all in place
and willing or not, each unit will grace
the presence of "I," like the rays do the sun,
and will, one day, know the Self to be One.

From Whole Self we come, so Whole Self we be,
one awareness - "I" - one Infinity;
for the Infinite is - the *full* presence of One,
emanating as "I," and even the crumb - -

must some day know that there's really no other,
than The "I" that is all, both father and mother,
and that the one "I" will continue to be,
expressing forever, more tangibly.

The time has come, to know that the "me,"
is not limited, like it seems to be
and that our real body is not made of sod
but of one "I," the awareness called "God."

THE TOUCH OF LOVE

The magical warmth of a finger's touch,
goes within, and does so much
to zero out the hurts and pains
that try to rule in silent domain.

The human creatures of loving caress
feel wind and rain on their sensitive flesh.
Is there even one, that understands
the aura of love in the touching of hands?

To be worthy of love - "to give and to take,"
and to know that love is here for our sake,
is a richness of being we try to address
through friendly concern and loving caress.

Love's in the touch of the wind in the trees -
and in the industrious hum of the bees;
and touching the heart of each species - held dear,
are its young, who gracefully live without fear.

Love is innate, and to most, mystery
but each knows within, their power "to be"
is a God-given Grace - a great gift of much -
including in it, the power to touch.

THE AURA OF LOVE

A touch of hand, or body, or speech
is truly sacred in those, whose reach
is not limited, to their own seed or breed -
and strives to fulfill what *everyone* needs.

Wisdom denies the "one" appetite
whose heart is aware, of the nations whose plight
includes starving masses - and the children who die -
their wings claimed by graves, before they can fly.

How can the belly of happiness thrive,
when masses struggle just to survive?
Who is it, that's callous to pain -
if not those, who live in the shame

of watching out for just "me and mine" -
with fun and games and T-V, held prime?
Blood seems so thick and all else so thin,
when we ignore the real meaning of "kin."

Is it not time for selective view
to look beyond the "selective few?"
The true touch of love has hardly begun
if it knows not, that all Self, is One.

The aura of love, in Truth, ever grows -
involving those, that as yet, don't know
it includes all - an infinite frame -
and they'll eventually realize the shame

of focussing in on just "me and mine,"
and will search for the path that's truly divine.
True compassion is playing its part,
to vanquish the fences surrounding our hearts.